STUDENT SUCCESS MANUAL to accompany

Understanding Human Communication

NINTH EDITION

RONALD B. ADLER
Santa Barbara City College

GEORGE RODMAN
Brooklyn College, City University of New York

Prepared by
Jeanne M. Elmhorst
Albuquerque TVI Community College

New York   Oxford
OXFORD UNIVERSITY PRESS
2006

Oxford University Press

Oxford University Press, Inc., publishes works that further Oxford University's
objective of excellence in research, scholarship, and education.

Oxford New York
Auckland   Cape Town   Dar es Salaam   Hong Kong   Karachi
Kuala Lumpur   Madrid   Melbourne   Mexico City   Nairobi
New Delhi   Shanghai   Taipei   Toronto

With offices in
Argentina   Austria   Brazil   Chile   Czech Republic   France   Greece
Guatemala   Hungary   Italy   Japan   Poland   Portugal   Singapore
South Korea   Switzerland   Thailand   Turkey   Ukraine   Vietnam

Copyright © 2006 by Oxford University Press, Inc.

Published by Oxford University Press, Inc.
198 Madison Avenue, New York, New York 10016
http://www.oup-usa.org

Oxford is a registered trademark of Oxford University Press

ISBN-13: 978-0-19-530487-9
ISBN: 0-19-530487-X

Printing number: 9 8 7 6 5 4 3 2 1

Printed in the United States of America
on acid-free paper

Table of Contents

LEARNING STYLES

People learn in different ways. Some understand best by reading (and re-reading), while others prefer listening to explanations. Still others get the most insight from hands-on experiences. Knowing your preferred way to take in and learn information can contribute to your college success. You might prefer to see information, to hear information, or to work with information in a hands-on way. In college you won't always be able to choose how information comes to you. Professors require lectures, textbooks, essays, labs, videos, and readings. In this section we'll help you understand your preferred learning style and help you discover ways to approach your studies that will work best for you.

In the next few pages we introduce five learning preferences and provide the opportunity for you to identify your own preference. Then you can put that information to work for you. There are many approaches to learning styles and preferences; here we present one of them, VARK, an acronym for Visual, Aural, Read/Write, and Kinesthetic ways of learning. A fifth category, multimodal, recognizes learners who have two or more strong preferences. No approach is better or worse than others; this is an opportunity to identify your learning preference and use that information to facilitate your college success.

The best way to begin is to identify your learning preference. You can do this by completing the following questionnaire.

The VARK Questionnaire

This questionnaire aims to find out something about your preferences for the way you work with information. You will have a preferred learning style, and one part of that learning style is your preference for the intake and output of ideas and information.

Choose the answer that best explains your preference and circle the letter next to it. Please circle more than one if a single answer does not match your perception. Leave blank any question that does not apply, but try to give an answer for at least ten of the thirteen questions

When you have completed the questionnaire, use the marking guide to find your score for each of the categories, Visual, Aural, Read/Write, and Kinesthetic. Then, to calculate your preference, use the scoring chart.

1. You are about to give directions to a person who is standing with you. She is staying in a hotel in town and wants to visit your house later. She has a rental car. You would

    a. draw a map on paper
    b. tell her the directions
    c. write down the directions (without a map)
    d. collect her from the hotel in my car

2. You are not sure if a word should be spelled "dependent" or "dependant." You would

    a. look it up in the dictionary
    b. see the word in my mind and choose by the way it looks
    c. sound it out in my mind
    d. write both versions down on paper and choose one

3. You have just received a copy of your itinerary for a world trip. This is of interest to a friend. You would

    a. phone her immediately and tell her about it
    b. send her a copy of the printed itinerary
    c. show her on a map of the world
    d. share what I plan to do at each place I visit

4. You are going to cook something as a special treat for your family. You would

    a. cook something familiar without the need for instructions
    b. thumb through the cookbook looking for ideas from the pictures
    c. refer to a specific cookbook where there is a good recipe

5. A group of tourists has been assigned to you to find out about wildlife reserves or parks. You would

    a. drive them to a wildlife reserve or park
    b. show them slides and photographs
    c. give them pamphlets or a book on wildlife reserves or parks
    d. give them a talk on wildlife reserves or parks

6. You are about to purchase a new stereo. Other than price, what would most influence your decision?

    a. the salesperson telling you what you want to know
    b. reading the details about it
    c. playing with the controls and listening to it
    d. it looks really smart and fashionable

7. Recall a time in your life when you learned how to do something like playing a new board game. Try to avoid choosing a very physical skill, like riding a bike. You learned best by:

    a. visual clues—pictures, diagrams, charts
    b. written instructions
    c. listening to somebody explaining it
    d. doing it or trying it

8. You have an eye problem. You would prefer the doctor to

   a. tell me what is wrong
   b. show me a diagram of what is wrong
   c. use a model to show me what is wrong

9. You are about to learn to use a new program on a computer. You would

   a. sit down at the keyboard and begin to experiment with the program's features
   b. read the manual which comes with the program
   c. telephone a friend and ask questions about it

10. You are staying in a hotel and have a rental car. You would like to visit friends whose address/location you do not know. You would like them to

    a. draw me a map on paper
    b. tell me the directions
    c. write down the directions (without a map)
    d. collect me from the hotel in their car

11. Apart from the price, what would most influence your decision to buy a particular book?

    a. I have read it before.
    b. A friend talked about it.
    c. I quickly read parts of it.
    d. The way it looks is appealing.

12. A new movie has arrived in town. What would most influence your decision to go (or not go)?

    a. I heard a radio review about it.
    b. I read a review about it.
    c. I saw a preview of it.

13. Do you prefer a lecturer or teacher who likes to use:

    a. a textbook, handouts, readings
    b. flow diagrams, charts, graphs
    c. field trips, labs, practical sessions
    d. discussion, guest speakers

The VARK Questionnaire—Scoring Chart

Use the following scoring chart to find the VARK category that each of your answers corresponds to. Circle the letters that correspond to your answers. For example, if you answered b and c for question 3, circle R and V in the question 3 row.

Question	a category	b category	c category	d category
3	A	R	V	K

Scoring Chart

Question	a category	b category	c category	d category
1	V	A	R	K
2	R	V	A	K
3	A	R	V	K
4	K	V	R	
5	K	V	R	A
6	A	R	K	V
7	V	R	A	K
8	A	V	K	
9	K	R	A	
10	V	A	R	K
11	K	A	R	V
12	A	R	V	
13	R	V	K	A

Calculating Your Scores

Count the number of each of the VARK letters you have circled to get your score for each VARK category.

Total number of **V**s circled =   (Visual score)

Total number of **A**s circled =   (Aural score)

Total number of **R**s circled =   (Read/write score)

Total number of **K**s circled =   (Kinesthetic score)

Calculating Your Preferences

Because you can choose more than one answer for each question, the scoring is complex. It can be likened to a set of four stepping stones across water.

1. Add up your scores: V + A + R + K =   (total)

2. Enter your scores from highest to lowest on the stones below, with their V, A, R, and K labels.

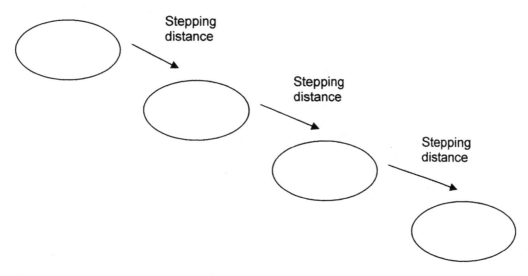

Stepping distance

Stepping distance

Stepping distance

3. Your stepping distance comes from this table.

Total of my four VARK scores is	My stepping distance is
10–16	1
17–22	2
23–26	3
More than 26	4

4. Your first preference is your highest score, so check the first stone as one of your preferences

5. If you can reach the next stone with a step equal to or less than your stepping distance, then check that one too. Once you can not reach your next stone, you have finished defining your set of preferences.

Now that you've scored your questionnaire, find the help sheet in the following pages that matches your preferred learning style. Go to the help sheet for each preference you have checked. If you have more than one preference checked, you should also read the material on multimodal preferences. Look at the specific strategies to study and learn (intake) information during class and independent study and then become familiar with and practice ways that will help you do well on exams (output). Read more about this resource for learning at www.vark-learn.com.

Visual Study Strategies

You want the whole picture, so you are probably holistic rather than reductionist in your approach. You are often swayed by the look of an object. You are interested in color, layout, and design, and you know where you are in your environment. You are probably going to draw something.

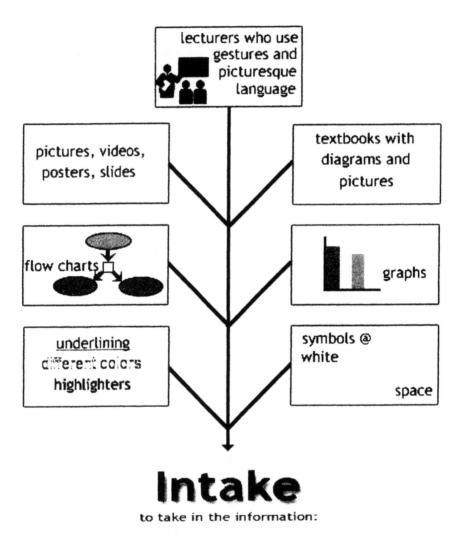

→ Use all the <u>techniques</u> above

Reconstruct the images in different ways
. . . try different spatial arrangements

Redraw your pages from memory

SWOT
STUDY WITHOUT TEARS

Replace words with symbols or initials

Look at your pages. ◉ ◉

Convert your lecture 'notes' into a learnable package
by reducing them $3:1$ into picture pages

⬇

Output
to perform well in the
examination:

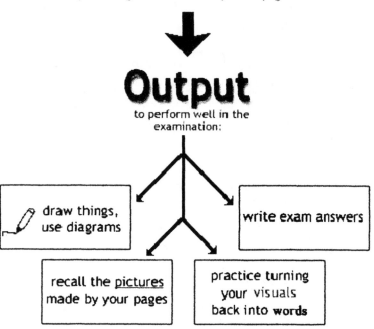

draw things,
use diagrams

write exam answers

recall the <u>pictures</u>
made by your pages

practice turning
your visuals
back into words

Aural Study Strategies

If you have a strong preference for learning by aural methods (**A** = hearing)**,** you should use some or all of the following:

> **INTAKE**
> To take in the information:

- Attend classes
- Attend discussions and tutorials
- Discuss topics with others
- Discuss topics with your teachers
- Explain new ideas to other people
- Use a tape recorder
- Remember the interesting examples, stories, and jokes
- Describe the overheads, pictures and other visuals to somebody who was not there
- Leave spaces in your notes for later recall and "filling"

> **SWOT—Study Without Tears**
> To make a learnable package:

Convert your notes into a learnable package by reducing them (3:1).

- Your notes may be poor because you prefer to listen. You will need to expand your notes by talking with others and collecting notes from the textbook.
- Put your summarized notes onto tapes and listen to them.
- Ask others to "hear" your understanding of a topic.
- Read your summarized notes aloud.
- Explain your notes to another "aural" person.

> **OUTPUT**
> To perform well in any test, assignment,
> or examination:

- Imagine talking with the examiner.
- Listen to your voices and write them down.
- Spend time in quiet places recalling the ideas.
- Practice writing answers to old exam questions.
- Speak your answers aloud or inside your head.

You prefer to have this entire page explained to you. The written words are not as valuable as those you hear. You will probably go and tell somebody about this.

Read/Write Study Strategies

If you have a strong preference for learning by reading and writing, you should use some or all of the following:

INTAKE
To take in the information:

- lists
- headings
- dictionaries
- glossaries
- definitions
- handouts
- textbooks

- readings—library
- notes (often verbatim)
- teachers who use words well and have lots of information in sentences and notes
- essays
- manuals (computing and laboratory)

SWOT—Study Without Tears
To make a learnable package:

Convert your notes into a learnable package by reducing them (3:1).

- Write out the words again and again.
- Read your notes (silently) again and again.
- Rewrite the ideas and principles into other words.
- Organize any diagrams, graphs, figures, or pictures into statements, for example,. "The trend is . . ."
- Turn reactions, actions, diagrams, charts, and flows into words.
- Imagine your lists arranged in multiple-choice questions and distinguish each from each.

OUTPUT
To perform well in any test, assignment, or examination:

- Write exam answers.
- Practice with multiple-choice questions.
- Write paragraphs, beginnings, and endings.
- Write your lists (a, b, c, d; 1, 2, 3, 4).
- Arrange your words into hierarchies and points.

You like this page because the emphasis is on words and lists. You believe the meanings are within the words, so any talk is okay, but this handout is better. You are heading for the library.

Kinesthetic Study Strategies

If you have a strong kinesthetic preference for learning, you should use some or all of the following:

> **INTAKE**
> To take in the information:

- all your senses—sight, touch, taste, smell, hearing
- laboratories
- field trips
- field tours
- examples of principles
- lecturers who give real-life examples
- applications
- hands-on approaches (computing)
- trial and error
- collections of rock types, plants, shells, grasses . . .
- exhibits, samples, photographs . . .
- recipes—solutions to problems, previous exam papers

> **SWOT—Study Without Tears**
> To make a learnable package:

Convert your notes into a learnable package by reducing them (3:1).

- Your lecture notes may be poor because the topics were not "concrete" or "relevant."
- You will remember the "real" things that happened.
- Put plenty of examples into your summary. Use case studies and applications to help with principles and abstract concepts.
- Talk about your notes with another kinesthetic person.
- Use pictures and photographs that illustrate an idea.
- Go back to the laboratory or your lab manual.
- Recall the experiments, field trips, etc.

> **OUTPUT**
> To perform well in any test, assignment,
> or examination:

- Write practice answers and paragraphs.
- Role play the exam situation in your own room.

You want to experience the exam so that you can understand it. The ideas on this page are only valuable if they sound practical, real, and relevant to you. You need to do things to understand.

Multimodal Study Strategies

If you have multiple preferences, you are in the majority, as somewhere between 50 and 70 percent of any population seems to fit into that group.

Multiple preferences are interesting and quite varied. For example, you may have two strong preferences, such as VA or RK, or you may have three strong preferences, such as VAR or ARK. Some people have no particular strong preferences, and their scores are almost even for all four modes. For example one student had scores of $V = 9$, $A = 9$, $R = 9$, and $K = 9$. She said that she adapted to the mode being used or requested. If the teacher or supervisor preferred a written mode, she switched into that mode for her responses and for her learning.

So, multiple preferences give you choices of two, three, or four modes to use for your interaction with others. Some people have admitted that if they want to be annoying, they stay in a mode different from the person with whom they are working. For example, they may ask for written evidence in an argument, knowing that the other person much prefers to refer only to oral information. Positive reactions mean that those with multimodal preferences choose to match or align their mode to the significant others around them.

If you have two dominant or equal preferences, please read the study strategies that apply to your two choices. If you have three or four preferences, read the three or four lists that apply. You will need to read two, three or four lists of strategies. For people with multimodal preferences it is necessary to use more than one strategy for learning and communicating. They feel insecure with only one. Alternatively, those with a single preference often "get it" by using the set of strategies that aligns with their single preference.

There seem to be some differences among those who are multimodal, especially those who have chosen fewer than seventeen options. If you have chosen fewer than seventeen of the options in the questionnaire you may prefer to see your highest score as your main preference—almost like a single preference. You are probably more decisive than those who have chosen seventeen-plus options.

Summary of VARK Scores

Now that you are familiar with your preferred learning style, come back to these pages and review the activities that will help you learn and process information best. Your favorite learning style may not match the teaching style used by the professor in this course. If that's the case, take the initiative to learn the material in the other ways outlined for you in the preceding pages while you continue to develop your ability to learn in ways that aren't your favored method.

Based on what you learned about your preferred learning method, list five specific things you can do to help yourself learn the material in this communication course.

1.

2.

3.

4

5.

STUDY SKILLS

Academic success doesn't just depend on how smart you are or how hard you work: it also depends on how *well* you study. Many students spend hours with their books but don't manage to understand the material they're expected to know. Not all methods of "spending time" with the text are equally productive, so we present here several methods that can help you study effectively.

Use SQ3R

SQ3R is a widely used acronym for an effective method to study a text. The method includes these five steps:

S-Survey
Q-Question
R-Read
R-Recite
R-Review

Survey

Begin by getting an overview of the material you'll later study in detail. Start with one chapter. Look at the title of the chapter and the major headings. Survey the opening page with its Chapter Highlights and objectives. Skim the chapter's tables, photos, cartoons, sidebars, figures, charts, and summaries. Glance at the Critical Thinking Probes and Ethical Challenges. At the end of each chapter, peruse the Key Terms, Activities, and Resources. This big-picture survey will help you put each section of the chapter in a larger context.

Question

Go back over the headings you have just surveyed and turn each one into a question. Most questions will include one of the following words: who, what, when, where, how, or why. Look how headings from *Understanding Human Communication* can fit into these forms:

- <u>Who</u> has power in groups? (Power in Groups, Chapter 9)
- <u>What</u> are the ways to help others when they have problems? (Empathic Listening, Chapter 4)
- <u>When</u> should you reveal personal information, and when should you keep it to yourself? (Guidelines to Appropriate Self-Disclosure, Chapter 6)
- <u>Where</u> can you find information for your speech? (Gathering Information, Chapter 10)
- <u>How</u> can you paraphrase? (Informational Listening, Chapter 4)
- <u>Why</u> is misunderstanding so common? (The Language of Misunderstandings, Chapter 3)

Read

Once you've reworded each section as a question, you can read the material to find an answer. Read only one section at a time so you can make sure you understand it before going on. As you answer a question, don't just rely on material in the text. Think about what you already know from your life experiences and from other classes.

Consider reading in a way that takes advantage of your strongest learning style. If your learning style is visual, highlight as you read, and translate what you read into pictures, drawings and diagrams in the margins or in your notes. If your learning style is aural, consider reading the book aloud, taping it, and then listening to the tape. If you learn best by reading/writing, you'll want to read all of the hand-outs and practice questions provided. If you're a kinesthetic learner, you'll learn by doing the activities on the CD ROM and completing the exercises at the end of each chapter. Review the specific strategies for your learning style presented in the preceding pages and use them.

Recite

After you've read the material, test your understanding by putting the ideas into your own words. Another word for reciting is <u>explaining</u>. Your goal here is to test your knowledge by rewording it. You can do this either in writing or by verbally explaining the material to a study partner, friend, or family member.

Reciting takes many forms; in fact, you'd be wise to use as many senses as you can. Consider using the techniques you learned in the VARK analysis. Are there some methods that work particularly well for your learning style? Now is the time to use them. If you're a visual learner, look up from your reading and recite what you've just learned by picturing the answer. Recall a visual from your notes and turn it into words. If you're an aural learner, speak your knowledge aloud and hear it in your own voice. If your preferred learning style is reading-writing, write the answer in your own words and read it in your own handwriting. If you are a kinesthetic learner, try to use all of your senses. Think of real life experiences and examples of what you're learning; act out concepts by actually practicing the skills in this course in various real situations. Most important in this step is translating information into your own words, not just memorizing someone else's words.

Review

Finally, review what you've learned by creating summarizing statements—either in full sentences or outlines. You can create review documents in short chunks (e.g., sections of a chapter) or on a chapter-by-chapter basis. These review documents can serve you well as you study for exams, so be sure to save them.

SQ3R is not a method to speed up studying like speed-reading techniques, and it is not a method for cramming the night before a final. It is a long-range approach to better understand and retain knowledge learned over the course of the semester. It is a method for studying texts that can help you succeed in this course if applied early and consistently. Learning in small segments and reviewing often results in greater learning and retention than cramming. We have inserted reminders to use this method in each chapter of this *Student Success Manual*.

Additional Study Ideas

Mark Your Texts

Forget the admonitions from your elementary teachers not to mark in your books. Studying is not a passive activity. You want to do more than just read your text; you want to study it, prepare for your exam, and increase your long-term retention of the information. When you mark your text you involve touch and movement, not just vision. This increased activity can stimulate brain activity and recall. Writing side notes to yourself, underlining, circling, and highlighting involve you in the process of learning. Here are some guidelines for marking your texts:

1. **Read before you mark.** In order to figure out what is most important, you need to read a paragraph or section before you mark it up. As you read, try to distinguish

main points from details. Analyze as you read to see categories and relationships of ideas. Before you mark, determine what is most important to focus on in order to review and remember.

2. **Develop a code of your own.** You might use circles for thesis statements and underlining for examples. When subpoints are spread out over several pages, you might use one color to highlight items of the same category. Use brackets, parenthesis, underlines, or quotation marks; develop a system that works for you. Improve your ability to spot the key ideas, relationships, causes and effects, and contrasts and similarities. If you need to, write down your code at the beginning of the chapter.

3. **Make notes in the margin.** Summarize a section in a few words of your own. Translate information into your way of talking and relate it to the lecture, another class or your personal life. Create a short outline or drawing in the margin to help you recall or relate information. Annotate for your benefit—do what helps you.

4. **Mark thoughtfully so you don't mark everything.** Marking more than 20 percent of the text defeats the purpose of distinguishing the key information to review later. Read first and think carefully about what to mark.

Choose Your Environment

Choose an effective setting in which to study. A successful study setting has minimal interruptions and distractions from external noise, other people, phones, televisions, and doorbells. A computer may help you take notes, organize your information, create study guides, and focus on the material you're learning or it might distract you with e-mail, instant messages, and surfing. It will take resolve not to answer the phone or check e-mail during your study time. Think about the physical environment of your study location and its comfort in terms of furnishings, lighting, and temperature. Consider furniture that is comfortable, but will not lull you to sleep. Chairs, desks and lighting should give you space and motivation to read and write. Keep the resources you need (paper, pencils, highlighters, dictionary) but not a lot more. Once you identify a place that works well for you to study, train yourself to use that place often so your brain associates serious study with that location. College libraries usually have well-designed, well-lit spaces with minimal distractions. The Study Environment Analysis (www.ucc.vt.edu/stdysk/ studydis.html) allows you to analyze study settings to determine the best environment for you.

Attend Study Sessions

If your professor or TA announces a study session, make it a priority to attend. These small sessions provide opportunities to review and ask questions. If study sessions are not sponsored by your professor, form a study group with other dedicated students.

Talking through the material, reviewing each other's notes, and quizzing each other will enhance your study skills and your comprehension and retention of the course concepts.

Seek Help

Familiarize yourself with your campus tutoring centers and labs, study skills workshops, student success centers, communication labs, supplemental instruction, peer mentoring, learning support services, learning assistance centers, or student learning centers. Check out resources to assist you in studying, writing assignments, and preparing for exams.

If you have a learning difficulty or disability, locate and use available services. The Office of Student Services (or the Office of Special Services) provides screening, diagnosing, and assistance for students with learning difficulties or special needs. If you already have documentation of a special need, take that to the appropriate office to receive services more quickly. If you think you may have dyslexia, Attention Deficit / Hyperactivity Disorder (ADHD), or any learning disability, you can arrange for a professional screening. After the screening, you can be referred for further testing or to other services to meet your needs. If you ask, colleges usually provide note-takers, books on tape, additional time for tests, and other reasonable accommodations for special needs.

Taking Notes in Class

The previous section offered advice for studying on your own. This section will help you understand the material that your professor presents in class. In addition to using the approaches for class lectures, you can also use them as a supplement or alternative to the SQ3R approach for better understanding the text and other readings. Two popular methods of note taking are the Cornell format and mind maps.

Cornell Note-Taking System

Taking notes while reading or while listening to a lecture occupies much of your time as a student. One tried-and-true method of note taking is the Cornell system. You can utilize this system with the following steps:

1. Before you begin to take notes, draw a vertical line down the left side of your paper about a fourth of the way over (2" from the left on an 8½" x 11" page).

2. As you listen for main points (see Chapter 4's section on informational listening), take notes on the right side.

3. Later, as you review your notes, put key words, significant phrases, and sample questions in the left column.

SAMPLE: Cornell Note-Taking System

2. Second, pull out key words and phrases and create questions here.	1. First, take notes on this side. Leave space to add to notes from text or readings. Focus on big ideas.
Group Interdependent What size is a small group? Hidden agenda	Groups are collections of individuals that interact over time and are interdependent. Usually between 3 and 20 people. Group members have common goals. Individual goals not shared with the group are called hidden agendas. (One person wants to make connections to get a new job—something just for him—but the group goal is to complete a report.)

Mind Mapping

Mind mapping is a technique you can use to take notes from a lecture or text and improve your recall of the ideas. A mind map is a visual representation of the material that emphasizes relationships of concepts. While an outline emphasizes linear relationships, a mind map (also called a concept map) shows associations, links and connections in a holistic way. An outline is more like a book; a mind map resembles information assembled as web links. Visual learners especially benefit from this method.

To construct your mind map, follow these guidelines:

1. Start in the middle of a large unlined sheet of paper.

2. Use only key words not sentences.

3. Use images (arrows, circles, sketches) that help you recall ideas and show relationships between words and groups of words.

4. Use colors to link related ideas and separate others.

5. Be creative.

A mind map of a lecture on listening might look like this:

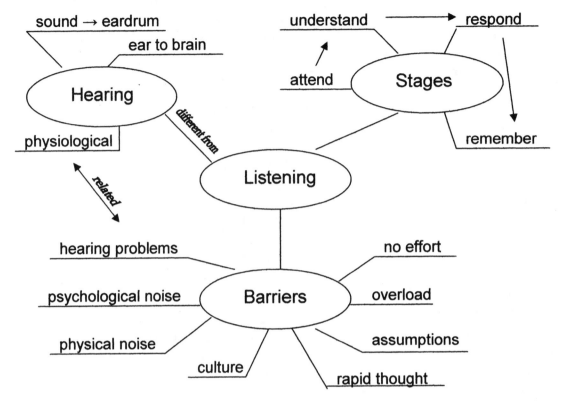

TEST-TAKING SKILLS

In most of your classes, you will take exams. Whether these are short, five-question quizzes or two-hour essay exams, here are some tips to improve your exam scores.

1. **Prepare for the exam you'll be given.** Read the syllabus carefully or talk with your instructor to find out what types of exams you'll take. Your text, this *Student Success Manual*, the *Student Resource Manual* CD-ROM, and the *Understanding Human Communication* Web site provide many tools to study for different kinds of exams. Ideally, you'll know the material well enough to be able to pass any type of exam; practically, you can use your time and energy to prepare most efficiently if you know the type of exam you'll be faced with. Here are some pointers for three common types of exam questions.

True/False

A. If the *whole* sentence isn't true, it isn't true. Conversely, if any part is false, it is false. Don't be thrown off by a partial truth buried in an otherwise false statement. Look for any falsehood.

B. Be aware of absolutes (always, never, only) and remember that if there is one exception, the question is false.

C. Statements phrased with negatives can be confusing. If changing it to a positive makes it true, the original sentence phrased as a negative is generally false. For example, "Nonverbal communication cannot be used to deceive." If you make this sentence a positive, it becomes "Nonverbal communication can be used to deceive." Since this is true, the opposite of the sentence must be false.

Multiple Choice

A. Read the first part of the question and think of the answer you would give if no choices were provided. Then see if that is one of the choices.

B. Before marking the answer, read all choices to be sure yours is the best. Most multiple-choice directions say choose the **best** answer, so all choices may be somewhat correct, but one might be better than the others. For instance, if you are choosing the best paraphrase, and one choice only paraphrases thoughts and another choice only paraphrases feelings, look for a *best* answer that paraphrases both thoughts and feelings. If a choice is more complete than others, it may be the best choice, even though others may be technically correct.

C. Check if "all (or none) of the above" is a choice. If you know for sure that two or three choices are correct (or incorrect), consider the "all (none) of the above" option.

D. Negative questions can be confusing. If the question is worded as a negative look at each option and mentally change the question to a positive. Then mark each choice that works. Generally, you will mark all but one and that one will be the correct answer for the original (negative) question. For example, "Which of the following is **not** a function of nonverbal communication?" can be mentally changed to "Which of these **is** a function of nonverbal communication?" If all but one choice correctly answers the second question, the unmarked question will generally be your answer to the original question.

E. If two choices seem too similar, re-read the question to be sure you understand what the question asks. Check carefully for some small difference in the answers, making one a better choice. Perhaps neither is correct; see if there is a better answer altogether.

Essay

A. Familiarize yourself with the types of words used in essays and be sure you understand their meaning. Commonly used words are describe, review, explain, compare, contrast, discuss, and evaluate. For each word, the instructor looks for a different reasoning process and type of answer. Read the question carefully and mark the words that tell you what type of answer is expected. Familiarize yourself with the definitions of twenty commonly used words found in essay questions at www.studygs.net/essay%20terms.htm.

B. Create an initial outline for each answer. Jot down an outline for each question, organizing your ideas around major themes that answer the question. State your thesis and your support. While you are writing one answer, if an idea pops into your head for another question, quickly add it to the outline.

C. Divide your time so that you answer each question. Your professor may give you partial credit for an outline or some sentences that show you understand the material, even if the grammar isn't correct and the thoughts aren't complete. Leaving a ten-point question blank results in losing ten points, no matter how extensive your answer to another question is.

D. Write neatly with space between your lines. This will allow you to go back and add information you think of later. If you are writing and you know the concept but can't think of the precise term or name, leave a blank, describe it, and fill it in later. You may think of it later or find it used in another part of the exam.

2. **Predict and prepare for likely types of test questions.** Use the outline provided in this *Student Success Manual* and the more extensive one in the *Student Resource Manual* on the CD-ROM to predict objective questions. For instance, if there are four steps or three characteristics listed, be prepared for a multiple-choice question that asks, "Which one of these is . . ." or "Which one of these is not . . ." Creating an outline or mind map from your lecture notes will help you predict questions on that material.

3. **Use practice questions effectively**. Use the *Student Resource Manual* CD-ROM to practice multiple-choice, true/false, fill-in-the-blank, and matching questions. Use this *Student Success Manual* to study for short-answer and synthesis questions. When using sample questions with an answer key, don't look at the answer key while answering the questions. If you simply tell yourself (after seeing the correct answer), "Yes, that's the answer I would have chosen," then using the sample exams will not

benefit you. Take the sample exams as actual exams without looking at the answers. Then go back and actually grade yourself. This reveals gaps in your knowledge and helps redirect your study time more productively.

4. **Arrive rested, early, and relaxed.** Be sure you've slept and eaten. Be comfortable and settled before the exam is handed out, with any necessary pens, pencils, and blue books at hand. Put away any unnecessary items so you're not distracted. If you can, relax your body by taking a few slow, deep breaths. Anxiety produces a body on "alert" that is not as capable of test taking as a calmer body.

5. **Plan your time.** Know how much each section of the exam is worth and then set up a time frame for yourself so you'll be able to spend the appropriate amount of time on each section. Check your time to be sure you're staying on task. If there is no penalty for guessing, then guess.

6. **Begin with what you know.** Peruse the exam and jot down ideas for questions you'll answer later. Then begin with the easy questions first to build confidence and get in the swing of things.

7. **Use the hints the exam provides.** Read carefully. Often the answer to one question is contained in another question. Stay alert to information that might be given. If one question is "List and describe the twelve major categories of Jack Gibb's theory of supportive and defensive communication" and another question is "Jack Gibb is best known for his theory of _____," the answer to the second is contained in the first.

8. **Analyze your exam to prepare for the next one.** Always learn from one exam so you can improve on the next one. An exam analysis is provided on the next page. Complete the exam analysis before you talk with your instructor and take it with you; it shows that you are serious about learning from exams, not just grubbing for points.

Postexam Analysis

After your exam, go through the exam and note the number of each item you missed, the code for the type of question you missed, the code for the reason you missed it, and any additional information that is important.

Come up with a plan to improve your studying and your exam scores.

Code for types of questions missed:

MC = Multiple Choice	**T/F** = True, False	**SA** = Short Answer
E = Essay	**FB** = Fill in the Blank	**M** = Matching

Code for reasons I missed items:

AB = Absent the day it was covered.

NN = Not in my notes, although I was there and took notes when it was explained.

N = It was in my notes, but I didn't study or comprehend it.

T = Answer was in the text; I didn't read it or didn't remember it.

MRQ = I misread the question. (reading error)

MUQ = I read the question but misunderstood what was asked. (comprehension error)

V = I didn't understand some of the general vocabulary used to ask the question.

DRC = I didn't read all choices; I picked one I thought was right without reading all.

H = I hurried to get to the end.

RCW = I had it right, erased it, and changed it to a wrong answer.

# Exam question missed	Code for type of question	Code for reason I missed the question	Additional, important information about the question or answer

Now go through your columns and see if you can determine a pattern. Did you miss mostly one type of question? Seek help for answering that type of question. Did you miss questions for one particular reason? What can you do to rectify that?

Write a paragraph in which you summarize what you learn from this analysis and create, in list or paragraph format, a plan to improve the skills you need to do better on the next exam.

WRITING

In addition to study and test-taking skills, your grades in college often hinge on your writing assignments. You've been learning to write for years, and in college it is especially important to apply all you've learned. Successful writing depends on your planning, development, organization, avoidance of plagiarism, and mastery of writing mechanics.

Planning

Read the assignment carefully and ask about anything you don't understand. Underline words on the assignment sheet that give requirements or planning details. Know the required length of the paper. Begin by clarifying your purpose so you know exactly why you are writing and who your audience is. Understand whether you are being asked to express an opinion, prove a point, analyze a situation, synthesize research, apply a theory, summarize an article, or accomplish some other purpose. Personal response or application papers are very different from book summaries, abstracts, or research papers. Determine whether your paper will be read only by your professor, by a panel, or by classmates as well. If you first know your purpose and your audience, you can plan more successfully. Write down your audience and purpose, and then sketch out a tentative thesis, outline, and possible supporting materials. See the step-by-step advice for planning major papers in "Timeline for a Term Paper" at the end of this section.

Development

Short opinion or analysis papers may not require outside research. They will, however, require that you develop your thoughts and support for your ideas carefully, but not necessarily with outside research. You will improve your development of any paper if you clarify your understanding of the types, functions, and styles of support explained in Chapter 11 of *Understanding Human Communication* ("Supporting Material"). While writing and speaking differ, the underlying principles and guidelines will serve you well in developing the types of support most appropriate to your paper. Whether you need to check a few facts or conduct extensive research, "Gathering Information" in Chapter 10 will help you develop your paper by using search engines, evaluating Web sites, and conducting library research.

Organization

Whether preparing papers or speeches, you'll do well to follow the guidelines for organization presented in Chapter 11 of *Understanding Human Communication*. Start with a thesis statement and carefully organize your main points and subpoints in a logical pattern. (See "Principles of Outlining" and "Organizing Your Points in a Logical Order.") Then structure your supporting material coherently for greatest impact. Use transitions in your paper as you would in a speech, to help readers understand the direction of your paper and how what you've already said relates to what comes next. (See "Using Transitions.") Finally, when your paper is largely written and you see your creation as a whole, it is time to write an introductory paragraph that gets the readers' attention, states the thesis, and previews the main points. Then write your conclusion so it reviews your thesis and main points and creates closure. Looking at the introduction and conclusion side by side helps you see whether your paper has unity and cohesion. (See "Beginning and Ending the Speech.")

Plagiarism

Virtually every student knows that cheating is a grave academic offense. Nobody who copies answers from a stolen test or a friend can claim ignorance of the rules as a defense. Plagiarism, though, isn't as well understood. Read your college's code of conduct or code of academic integrity to see its definition of academic dishonesty and plagiarism. Here is a breakdown of the most widely recognized types of plagiarism.

Copying

Replicating another person's work word-for-word is plagiarism. This includes any format or activity that involves taking someone else's work (for example, their paper, speech, cartoon, or exam) and presenting it as your own in any form (report, speech, or paper). If you are quoting someone else directly in writing, indicate their words in quotation marks and properly cite the source. An English handbook will show you how to do citations. In speaking, use an oral citation to clarify the words and the source. Sometimes, plagiarism results from hurried or careless research if you later cannot determine whether your note cards contain a summary in your own words or quotations from your source. Avoid this by consistently using quotation marks appropriately and carefully coding your notes.

Paraphrasing

Even if you put others' writings in your own words, you must credit the source. If the words are largely your own paraphrase, but include key words and phrases from another source, put the key words and phrases in quotation marks and cite the source.

Using ideas

Even though you are not quoting or paraphrasing, credit the source of an idea. The exception is information that is common knowledge and is found without credits in multiple quality sources. For instance, almost all communication texts list many types of nonverbal communication, including a category about how far or close we interact with each other. This category, called proxemics, is common knowledge and needs no citations. However, if you describe the distances at which we interact as "intimate, personal, social, and public," those are the words and ideas of Edward T. Hall, and his work would need to be cited.[1]

Drawing on nonprint sources

The basis of your writing might be a movie, television show, radio broadcast, or Web site. If ideas, paraphrases, or quotations come from these, be sure to cite them. Style guides and English handbooks give you formats for doing so.

In brief, credit those who shape your research and ideas. In the process, your citations demonstrate that you've researched and studied beyond your text. You get credit for researching and enhance your credibility when you cite quality work. Be sure to do your own synthesizing, analyzing, and reflecting on your research so that your thesis and writing reflects your own thinking and is not just a series of quotations strung together. The ideas, organization, and particular process of asking and answering a research question should be yours. Demonstrate that you have original thoughts, interpretations, analyses, and means of expression supported by current research and experts.

Grammar and Mechanics

No matter how brilliant your thoughts are, grammatical and mechanical errors create "noise" for the grader so that your ideas get lost. Use complete sentences to create coherent paragraphs. A spelling and grammar check on your computer helps, but it misses many types of errors, so don't rely solely on it. Use the online and in-person resources available to you to review grammar and spelling concerns. After you proofread, have a tutor or competent friend read your paper to see if it makes sense, is readable, and is free of errors. Double-check that your paper adheres to specific requirements with regard to acceptable font style and size, spacing, margins, and style (APA or MLA).

---

[1] E. Hall, *The Hidden Dimension* (Garden City, NY: Anchor Books, 1969).

Checklist for Your Paper

Reviewing this checklist might improve your paper and your grade. Does your paper:

☐ get your readers' attention in the opening paragraph?

☐ state your thesis and preview your main points in your opening paragraph?

☐ present ideas in an organized and logical manner?

☐ sound coherent? Do ideas make sense and hang together?

☐ have a topic sentence in each paragraph and other complete sentences that logically follow to make a point?

☐ develop ideas with adequate support for the points made?

☐ use transitions to help the reader understand the movement from one idea to another?

☐ have an interesting and summative conclusion that reviews the main points and brings closure?

☐ use the required sources (kind and number)?

☐ cite all sources in the proper style?

☐ mark direct quotations appropriately?

☐ credit paraphrases and ideas of others?

☐ have no spelling and grammar errors?

☐ include a cover page (if required) with title, your name, professor's name, course number and section, and date?

☐ conform to the deadline?

☐ adhere to requirements for length, spacing, fonts, and any additional instructions on the assignment sheet?

Timeline for a Term Paper

Putting off a writing assignment is a plan for disaster. It's not likely that you can put together a decent paper if you start a day or two before the deadline. Use a calendar or day planner to plot the day the assignment is due and then work backward to design a workable timeline of activities needed to complete the paper. For a term paper, create a semester plan. Adjust your timetable accordingly for shorter writing assignments that may not require as much research. Always allow time to revise and rewrite. The Assignment Calculator (www.lib.umn.edu/help/calculator) prompts you to plug in the date your paper is due and displays a day-planner guide to work on this assignment. Each step of the way you can click on tools to help you organize your thoughts, create a plan, and locate detailed tips.

As you proceed, save your work frequently, and always make a copy of your work so you never lose all of it. Too many students have learned this lesson the hard way with a low grade to prove it.

For a research paper due the 14th week of the term, your timeline might look like this:

Weeks 2 – 3

- ✓ **Know your assignment**. Read the assignment carefully and ask questions if you are not sure what the process and the final product should look like.

- ✓ **Update your research skills**. Students are often unaware of the resources in their university library. What resources—journals, books, databases, special collections —do you have access to? Don't think you have to discover these on your own: Get to know the reference librarian and ask for help.

- ✓ **Choose your topic.** If the professor is assigning topics, get yours as early as you can. If there is a list to choose from, pick yours early. If the topic is your choice, make sure your instructor agrees that it fits the assignment. See Chapter 10 of *Understanding Human Communication* for advice on choosing a topic. When you've identified a likely topic, do a quick search to see if there seems to be enough information. Narrow your topic. Make sure it fits the assigned length of the project.

Weeks 4 – 5

- ✓ **Develop a research question** that specifically asks the question you are trying to answer through your research. Careful wording of the question helps you organize and plan your research and, later, your writing.

- ✓ **Clarify the kinds of research required**. Professors may allow only scholarly (peer-reviewed) journals or may require a certain number or percentage be scholarly. The number and type of web sites allowed may be limited. Know before you begin so you use your time wisely.

✓ **Devise your research strategy** by working with a reference librarian to find the information you need. Ask about indexes, catalogs, databases, and Internet resources. Keep records of the sources (databases, key words, Web sites) you've researched so you don't duplicate your efforts.

✓ **Critically review and evaluate your sources.** See Web references in the Internet Resources section to help you with this.

✓ **Take notes and create a working outline.** Careful notes help you avoid plagiarism and clarify what is or isn't another person's work. Be consistent with a system to identify whether you have exact quotes, paraphrases, or ideas from another person.

✓ **Record your sources in the required format** so that you can properly cite them in your references or works cited list. Know what style is required for your final paper and cite your sources in that format now. This saves hours of backtracking later to find a part of the citation you'd forgotten. Most communication courses will use APA or MLA styles; references for both are in the Internet Resources section on page 31.

✓ **Broaden or narrow your topic** depending on the amount of information you find.

Weeks 7 – 9

✓ **Create a thesis statement and outline**. When you have much of the information you need, develop a thesis and main points in complete sentences and note where your research will be inserted to develop your points. Your outline helps you see what pieces of information are missing and what sections require more research.

✓ **Continue your research** to round out your paper.

Weeks 10 – 11

✓ **Begin writing** when you have all of your information and your outline. As you write, focus on answering your research question.

✓ **Follow the technical requirements** for the paper. Read the assignment or check with the professor to be certain about the spacing, font size, margins, style (APA or MLA), and cover required.

✓ **Revise and rewrite.** Allow time to seek help from your professor, TA, writing lab, or tutor. Be certain to print a hard copy and create a backup of everything at this point. Back up your work each time you revise.

Weeks 12 – 13

✓ **Proofread**. Ask others to read your paper for coherence and errors.

✓ **Finish** your paper at least two days before the due date to allow for computer crashes and printer problems. Print a copy and proofread the hard copy. This also guarantees having something in hand should you experience a technology failure.

CLASSROOM CIVILITY

You'll be more successful in this and other classes if you accept the responsibilities that come with being a student.

1. **Know the rules of the course.** Check your syllabus; it generally spells out what you can expect in the class and what's expected of you. Since no two classes have identical rules, you can save yourself grief and boost the odds of success by investing time in reading that syllabus. Some professors even give a pop quiz on the contents of the syllabus.

2. **Attend each class.** Attendance plays an important part in college success and students who don't skip class have several advantages: they hear explanations of assignments and changes in assignments, due dates, or test dates. They hear test reviews, they can ask questions, and they often gain an edge if a grade is borderline. Attendance attests to your seriousness as a student and your willingness to take responsibility for your learning. In a communication class such as this, participation in class activities often accounts for both learning the skills and is part of the assessment (grade) for the course.

3. **Show up on time**. In some cultures and some high schools, being tardy is accepted, but the culture of college classrooms is that classes start on time and you're tardy (or marked absent) if you're not there for the start of class.

4. **Come prepared**. Check the syllabus and be sure you read the assigned chapters before class. You'll be prepared for quizzes, activities based on the reading, and lectures. You'll also understand more from the lectures.

5. **Accept responsibility: What you do (and don't do).** If you're absent from a class, find out what you missed from your professor or other students before the next meeting and do what's necessary to stay caught up. If the syllabus clearly tells you to check the Web site and not to contact the professor to find out what you've missed, follow that advice. Turn in work on time. If an assignment is late, acknowledge that fact. Excuses usually won't impress your professor, who has probably heard them all before.

   Another way to accept responsibility is to avoid the "you" language described in Chapter 7. For example, instead of attacking your professor by saying, "You didn't explain this very well," use "I" language and say, "I didn't understand . . ."

6. **Behave in a civil manner.** Since you don't want to antagonize your professor and fellow students, follow the basic rules of civil behavior in groups. Show up on time to class. Turn off your cell phone and pager. Don't hold side conversations or butt into a lecture or discussion without being recognized first.

7. **Show your interest.** Even if you aren't constantly fascinated by what's happening in class, acting the part of an interested student will make a good impression; and often acting interested may even help you feel more engaged. Nonverbal indicators that you are interested include leaning forward, making eye contact, smiling, nodding responsively and appropriately, asking sincere and thoughtful questions, and volunteering for activities if asked. These behaviors will likely enhance your own learning and that of your classmates. In addition, you will help to create a supportive classroom climate.

   Ask questions. If you don't understand, ask. Ask in a way that does not create defensiveness or take unnecessary class time. If something has been explained, try to identify the specific point you don't understand, rather than ask for the whole topic to be repeated. Specific questions, such as asking the professor to differentiate between two points, "Could you explain when self-concept and self-esteem are different?" or asking for an example, "Could you give an example of how self-concept and self-esteem differ?" will help you more than a general request like, "Can you go over self-concept and self-esteem again?" As you study, prepare questions that delve deeper into the material, questions that will help you understand. If you feel uncomfortable or if there is no opportunity to ask in class, try to ask the professor after class, during office hours, or by e-mail. The important thing is to ask.

   Avoid behaviors that say you're *not* interested in class: text-messaging, reading another book, talking, rummaging through your pack or purse, putting your head down, sleeping, and so forth. You get the picture.

8. **Treat others with respect in class discussions.** Listen to other points of view. Part of classroom civility is hearing and responding appropriately to others' opinions. Classrooms are marketplaces of ideas; prepare to hear and listen to opinions different from yours.

   Understand others before responding. Before you respond to someone else, be sure you've understood his or her point of view. Use perception checks (Chapter 2) and paraphrases (Chapter 4) to clarify what the other has said before you respond. Use these skills to ensure that you don't embarrass yourself with a lengthy disagreement, only to find that you misunderstood the point.

   In your own comments, avoid acting dogmatically when you are actually expressing your opinion. Rather than saying, "Women are . . ." or "Men are . . .," use the phrase, "In my opinion, women are . . ." or "In my experience, men are . . ." This shows you understand the difference between facts, opinions, and inferences—concepts covered in Chapter 3. Other phrases that can help you be clear about recognizing that what you are saying is your own opinion, not absolute fact, are "I have learned . . .," "I have come to believe . . .," "I am convinced . . .," or "I have concluded . . ." This sort of language is less likely to trigger defensiveness than dogmatic statements. You can help reduce defensiveness and build a positive communication climate (Chapter 7).

9. **Stay positive**. Approach the class with a positive attitude and, even when frustrated, don't take your frustration out on the professor or other students. Stating that you're frustrated is okay but unnecessary. Stating, "I want to be sure I understand this. I want to learn this" are positive affirmations for you, your professor, and your classmates. You will generally get a more positive reaction than if you begin on a negative note like, "This is really hard. I don't know how you expect us to remember all these key terms." Focus on your goals. If your goal is to learn and to understand, stay focused on that. For more details about positive thinking benefits for students, see www.marin.cc.ca.us/~don/Study/Hcontents.html.

10. **Recognize that success takes work.** Joining a class is like signing up for a gym membership; even though you're a "customer," you will only benefit if you follow the plan your coach (i.e., your professor) sets out for you. Commit to showing up for your classes (workouts) ready to do what it takes to tone up your understanding.

How well are you doing? Use the Classroom Savvy Checklist to find out. www.mtsu.edu/~studskl/savylist.htm.

INTERNET RESOURCES

Attention Deficit Disorder

Causes, characteristics, treatment, and legal issues plus strategies for coping, studying, and learning: www.ucc.vt.edu/stdysk/addhandbook.html

Attitude

www.marin.cc.ca.us/~don/Study/Hcontents.html

Avoiding Plagiarism

www.georgetown.edu/honor/plagiarism.html#country
www.indiana.edu/~wts/pamphlets/plagiarism.shtml

Classroom Saavy Checklist

www.mtsu.edu/~studskl/savylist.htm

Cornell Note Taking

www.bucks.edu/~specpop/Cornl-ex.htm

Evaluating Sources

http://owl.english.purdue.edu/workshops/hypertext/EvalSrcW/index.html

Learning Styles

www.vark-learn.com

Marking Texts

www.utexas.edu/student/utlc/handouts/1420.html

Mind and Concept Mapping

How to mind map with sample: www.mindtools.com/mindmaps.html
How to mind map: www.peterussell.com/MindMaps/HowTo.html
Outline/example of mind mapping: www.bucks.edu/~specpop/sem-map.htm
Examples of web, tree, chart, chain, sketch:
     www.bucks.edu/~specpop/vis-org-ex.htm#web
Concept mapping:
     www.utc.edu/Administration/WalkerTeachingResourceCenter/FacultyDevelopme
     nt/ConceptMapping/index.html#what-is
Concept mapping homepage: http://users.edte.utwente.nl/lanzing/cm_home.htm

Overcoming Procrastination Self-Help Program

www.utexas.edu/student/utlc/makinggrade/pselfhelp.html

SQ3R

www.ucc.vt.edu/lynch/TextbookReading.htm.
www.studygs.net/texred2.htm
www.arc.sbc.edu/sq3r.html,
www.teach-nology.com/web_tools/graphic_org/sq3r/

Study Environment Analysis

www.drake.edu/provost/acadsuccess/TableOfContents/Studying/StudyEnv.htm
www.ucc.vt.edu/stdysk/studydis.html

Test-Taking Skills

Essay: www.studygs.net/essay%20terms.htm

Writing Assistance

www.ucc.vt.edu/stdysk/termpapr.html
http://webster.commnet.edu/mla/index.shtml
http://owl.english.purdue.edu/handouts/index.html

Writing Papers

www.lib.umn.edu/help/calculator

Writing Styles

APA: www.wisc.edu/writetest/Handbook/DocAPAReferences.html
MLA: http://webster.commnet.edu/mla/index.shtml

CHAPTER 1 HUMAN COMMUNICATION: WHAT AND WHY

SQ3R in Action

Generate an SQ3R chart for this chapter here: www.teach-nology.com/web_tools/ graphic_org/sq3r/

Survey

Skim the title, Chapter Highlights, objectives ("You should understand" and "You should be able to"), headings, tables, photos, cartoons, figures, charts, and items in the margin. Glance at the titles of the Critical Thinking Probes and Ethical Challenges. At the end of each chapter, look over the list of Key Terms, Activities, and Resources.

Question

Ask yourself questions. What do you know about these topics from your own life experiences and from other classes? Ask these six questions in each section: who, what, when, where, how, and why.

Read

Take one heading at a time and read to find the answers to the questions you've posed.

Recite

In your own words, say the answer aloud and then write it out.

Review

Review each section and then review the whole chapter. This is a good time to use the activities at the end of each chapter and the activities and the sample exams on the CD-ROM. Remember to periodically review the previous chapters as well.

Chapter 1 Outline

(Italicized words are key terms.)

I.   Human *communication* is the process of responding to others' symbolic behavior.
  A. Communication is human; in this text we do not consider machine and animal communication.
  B. Communication is a continuous, transactional process.
  C. Communication is symbolic (uses *symbols* that represent other things).
II. Types of communication include intrapersonal, dyadic or interpersonal, small group, public, and mass communication.
III. Communication satisfies physical, identity, social, and practical needs.

IV. The *transactional model* is more accurate than the *linear model* of communication.
    A. The elements of a linear model *(sender,* message, *receiver, noise, environment, channel*—includes *mediated communication)* are valid, but its one-way nature is not.
    B. The transactional model more accurately portrays communication as a simultaneous, fluid, relational process of *decoding* and *encoding.*
V. A competent communicator both **understands** and **demonstrates** proficiency.
    A. *Communication competence* isn't a single, ideal way of communicating; it is situational and relational and can be learned.
    B. Competent communicators carefully choose and skillfully enact the most appropriate behavior while demonstrating empathy, cognitive complexity, self-monitoring, and commitment to the relationship.
VI. Correcting these common misconceptions about communication leads to greater satisfaction.
    A. Communication doesn't always require complete understanding; *coordination* may be sufficiently satisfying.
    B. Communication is not always a good thing.
    C. No single person or event causes another's reaction.
    D. Communication will not solve all problems.
    E. Meanings are in people, not in words.
    F. Communication is not simple; it is complex.
    G. More communication is not always better.

Chapter 1 Summary

Human communication relies on symbols. Symbols may be words, nonverbal behavior, looks, clothing or anything that represents something other than itself. When one human being responds to another person's symbols, communication occurs. Additionally, human communication can occur in many contexts including within oneself (intrapersonal), between two people (dyads), face-to-face (interpersonal), in small groups, in public settings, or as mass communication.

Communication is a transactional process, meaning that people are sending and receiving messages simultaneously. They are observing and responding to each other at the same time, whether that response is verbal or nonverbal, observable or not. It is a constant process and difficult to determine where it begins and ends. We study communication because we use it every day to meet our needs. We meet physical needs such as health needs, identity needs such as letting others know who we are and what we value, social needs such as feeling included and being respected, and practical needs such as getting and keeping a job, renting an apartment, or filling an order at the pharmacy.

How do we know if someone is a competent communicator? Who decides what competence is? Who evaluates competence? If we examine these questions, we see that competence requires knowing what is proficient and being able to do it. In communication, there often isn't one right answer, one right way to do something. After learning skills, each communicator must evaluate the situation (context) and the relationship (who is communicating with whom) and choose to use the skills needed for this particular situation. Competent communicators choose their behaviors from a wide repertoire of skills and demonstrate concern for others (empathy), an ability to see events from others' perspectives (cognitive complexity), and the capacity to observe and evaluate their own behaviors (self-monitoring). Commitment to the relationship rounds out the necessary tools of competent communicators.

Because we may have received some inaccurate messages about the nature, power, and realities of communication, clearing up some misconceptions helps us approach the study of communication more accurately. People don't have to completely understand each other for communication to be effective or satisfying. For instance, couples may not totally understand their partner's reasons for enjoying certain sports or voting for certain candidates, but they may be content to have a realization of their differences and a system of meeting each other's needs and coordinating their behaviors without completely understanding the other. More communication does not automatically result in greater relational satisfaction, nor will communication solve all problems. For instance, if someone is greedy or has a physiological addiction or a brain disorder, all of the communication in the world may not solve these issues. At any given time, more communication may not produce a better result. Because communication is so complex, there is often more than one cause for anyone's reaction. The meaning of any utterance or event is not in the words used, but in the people choosing and using the words.

These fundamentals of communication form the foundation for the more complex concepts presented in the next chapters.

Chapter 1 Key Terms

For each of these terms, define the term, give an example, and explain the significance of the term.

1. channel

2. communication

3. communication competence

4. coordination

5. decode

6. dyad

7. dyadic communication

8. encode

9. environment

10. feedback

11. interpersonal communication

12. intrapersonal communication

13. linear communication model

14. mass communication

15. mediated communication

16. noise

17. public communication

18. receiver

19. sender

20. small group communication

21. symbol

22. transactional communication model

Chapter 1 Review Questions

These questions are designed to help you understand this chapter's concepts and express your understanding in your own words. For practice with true/false and multiple-choice questions, use the CD-ROM you received with the text.

1. In your own words, define communication and identify the key characteristics of communication.

2. Give an example of each of the five types of communication identified in this text.

3. Give original examples of the four needs that can be satisfied by communication.

4. Differentiate between linear and transactional communication models.

5. What is communication competence, and how would you recognize a competent communicator?

6. What are seven common misconceptions with regard to communication? Give an example of what can result from each of these misconceptions.

7. How would you rate your communication competence, and what can you do to improve it?

Chapter 1 Thinking Outside the Box: Synthesizing Your Knowledge

These questions are designed to help you develop the big picture by blending what you've learned in this chapter and elsewhere.

1. What proverbs, family admonitions, sayings, and teachings have you learned from your family, community, religion, culture, and experiences that support or refute the notion of a competent communicator as presented in the text?

2. How do concepts in this chapter compare and contrast to ideas you may have learned in biology, psychology, sociology, or business classes?

Chapter 1 Answers to Review Questions

1. In your own words, define communication and identify the key characteristics of communication.

    As defined and studied in this text, the definition of communication includes the terms "human," "process," and "symbolic behavior." All are part of the process (not a solo act) involved when humans respond to the symbols (language and nonverbal behavior) used by others.

2. Give an example of each of the five types of communication identified in this text.

    Examples will vary with personal experience and knowledge. Sample answers might include the following:

    a) *Intrapersonal: Your answers should involve one person talking to him- or herself, mulling over a decision, thinking, communicating with himself internally.*
    b) *Dyadic/interpersonal: Your answer should show at least two people communicating, paying attention to each other and responding to each other. Examples: talking with my mom or a classmate; four friends discussing their upcoming trip together.*
    c) *Small group: Your answer should include a group of three or more people interacting to reach a common goal such as your soccer team or your assigned small group for a class presentation*
    d) *Public: Your answer should show one person speaking to a large audience with limited feedback, such as an instructor lecturing to a section of over two hundred students.*
    e) *Mass: Your answer should show a mediated channel reaching large numbers of people, such as a television ad for a political candidate.*

3. Give original examples of the four needs that can be satisfied by communication.

   1. *Physical: asking your landlord to turn on the heat or participating in a support group such as Alcoholics Anonymous.*
   2. *Identity: wearing a Green Bay Packers shirt when attending an out-of-town game.*
   3. *Social: sending letters to new members of an organization inviting them to a potluck, hoping they feel included.*
   4. *Practical: sitting down with new roommates to decide who will take out the garbage, pay the gas bill, and so forth.*

4. Differentiate between linear and transactional communication models.

   Linear models view communication as a straight line, something that happens in one direction as a sender sends a message to a receiver; encoding and decoding are discrete operations. The more accurate transaction model emphasizes the fact that one is sender and receiver at the same time, encoding and decoding simultaneously since communication is relational (not individual). Both models include channels, noise and environment.

5. What is communication competence, and how would you recognize a competent communicator?

   A competent communicator has many behaviors available to him or her, chooses the best behavior, and skillfully enacts it. A competent communicator behaves in the most appropriate way, one that respects the feelings of others, understands a variety of points of view, looks at and analyzes his or her own behavior, and expresses commitment to rather than apathy toward the relationship.

6. What are seven common misconceptions with regard to communication? Give an example of what can result from each of these misconceptions.

   1. *Communication doesn't always require complete understanding; coordination may be sufficiently satisfying. "How are you?" may be a ritual or cliché conversation that doesn't require either person to totally understand the other.*
   2. *Communication is not always a good thing. In an emergency situation, a trained medical person finds it better to act quickly than take time to communicate about what she's doing.*
   3. *No single person or event causes another's reaction. Although my mom yelled at me and is frustrated that I'm not spending holidays with the family, my actions alone didn't cause her reaction. Her expectations, beliefs, and my sister being overseas added to her response.*
   4. *Communication will not solve all problems. My cousin is addicted to drugs, and communication won't solve the physical addiction.*

5. *Meanings are in people, not in words. My British friend uses the phrase, "All right then" when things aren't going well, but I often interpret it to mean that all is well with the situation.*

6. *Communication is not simple; it is complex. Trying to teach dance to a group of fourth graders reminds me that each comes with a different perception of dance, a different idea of who they are and what they need from this dance group, and a different ability level to respond to my requests.*

7. *More communication is not always better. I wanted my parents to decide whether they'd pay my tuition for graduate school at the moment I first asked them; they wanted to think it over. Insisting on more talk about it right then and there did not bring a better outcome.*

7. How would you rate your communication competence, and what can you do to improve it?

   Your answers will vary greatly, applying some of the principles in this chapter. For instance, you might analyze your communication competence based on the elements of the model, the concepts that make up a competent communicator, or the misconceptions you could be operating under.

Chapter 1 Answers to Thinking Outside the Box

1. What proverbs, family admonitions, sayings and teachings have you learned from your family, community, religion, culture, and experiences that support or refute the notion of a competent communicator as presented in the text?

   Answers will vary widely. Ideas include proverbs such as "You'll catch more flies with honey than with vinegar," which might have taught someone to use kind words rather than harsh ones. Or "Don't beat around the bush," which might have taught someone to be very direct.

2. How do concepts in this chapter compare and contrast to ideas you may have learned in biology, psychology, sociology, or business classes?

   Consider what you may have learned in biology about genetic sources of communication and personality. Perhaps you've studied Pavlov's experiment in psychology and see how that relates to learning communication skills. Did sociology reveal how we learn to communicate based on race or class? Did business classes teach you which communication channels to use in certain situations? Did you study Maslow's Hierarchy of Needs in psychology?

CHAPTER 2 PERCEPTION, THE SELF, AND COMMUNICATION

SQ3R in Action

Generate an SQ3R chart for this chapter here: www.teach-nology.com/web_tools/graphic_org/sq3r/

Survey

Skim the title, Chapter Highlights, objectives ("You should understand" and "You should be able to"), headings, tables, photos, cartoons, figures, charts, and items in the margin. Glance at the titles of the Critical Thinking Probes and Ethical Challenges. At the end of each chapter, look over the list of Key Terms, Activities, and Resources.

Question

Ask yourself questions. What do you know about these topics from your own life experiences and from other classes? Ask these six questions in each section: who, what, when, where, how, and why.

Read

Take one heading at a time and read to find the answers to the questions you've posed.

Recite

In your own words, say the answer aloud and then write it out.

Review

Review each section and then review the whole chapter. This is a good time to use the activities at the end of each chapter and the activities and the sample exams on the CD-ROM. Remember to periodically review the previous chapters as well.

Chapter 2 Outline

(Italicized words are key terms.)

I. Our own *narratives*, perceptual tendencies, situational factors, culture, and degree of empathy all shape our perceptions and consequently, our communication.

    A. By telling our stories, our narratives help us make sense of the world; creating shared narratives with others enhances our mutual communication.

    B. Common but often inaccurate perceptual tendencies influence us.

        1. judging ourselves more charitably than others *(self-serving bias)*

        2. paying attention to obvious stimuli

        3. clinging to first impressions

           4.   assuming others are similar to us

           5.   favoring negative impressions

           6.   blaming victims

   C. We perceive others and ourselves in light of situational factors, such as our relational satisfaction, level of involvement, past experiences, expectations, social roles, knowledge, and self-concept.

   D. Culture influences perception by providing different filters, such as the value of talk and silence, eye contact, and other nonverbal behaviors.

   E. *Empathy* is a blend of taking another's cognitive and emotional perspective with having genuine concern for the other.

           1.   Empathy differs from *sympathy,* which involves compassion, not identification.

           2.   A *perception check* helps determine the accuracy of perception by describing behavior, stating two possible interpretations, and requesting clarification.

II. One's *self-concept* shapes perceptions of self and others and influences communication with others.

   A. Self-concept is our view of our own characteristics while *self-esteem* is our judgment or evaluation of our characteristics.

   B. Reflected appraisal by significant others shapes one's identity.

   C. Cultures impact self-concept through language, names, and values and by emphasizing and rewarding different behaviors.

   D. *Personality,* which appears to be at least partly innate, influences both self-concept and communication.

   E. *Self-fulfilling prophecies* exert a powerful, positive or negative influence on communication, whether they are self-constructed prophecies or those constructed by others.

III. Identity management *(impression management)* is a process of trying to shape others' views of oneself.

   A. Since the *perceived self* (honest, private perception of self) sometimes differs from the *face* or *presenting self* (the public image you want others to have of you), many of our behaviors are attempts at impression management or *facework* (efforts to manage our own identities and reinforce those presented by others).

   B. Much identity management includes multiple identities that are collaboratively constructed, either deliberately or unconsciously.

   C. We manage impressions to agree with social rules, roles, and personal goals.

   D. In face-to-face impression management, manner, appearance, and setting help shape others' impressions; in mediated contexts, persons exert different kinds of control over different parts of the impression management process.

   E. Impression management is honest or dishonest and involves ethical choices.

Chapter 2 Summary

The way we perceive ourselves and present ourselves to others is an integral part of interpersonal communication. It impacts how we communicate to others and how we perceive communication from others.

We manage our identities in various ways in order to maintain the presenting self, or face, that we want others to see. This varies from one context to another. You might want your supervisor to see you as a hard worker who is always on time; you might want your coworkers to see you as empathic and flexible. Managing your identity can take many forms: setting, manner, and appearance. Different faces can be completely honest because each of us embodies many different characteristics simultaneously and consistently. However, it is important to be aware of the ethical dimensions of self-presentation. Consider when the presentation of different faces is honest and ethical and when adding or omitting information to create a certain identity would violate ethical principles of rightness, fairness, and honesty.

We are more effective at identity management if we first understand our self-concept, those stable characteristics we see in ourselves. Our view of ourselves develops from the many reflected appraisals we receive from significant others, particularly early in our lives. What they communicate to us shapes our view of ourselves. Then, our own self-esteem develops from the value we place on the characteristics we see in ourselves. The culture we live and interact in influences our view of ourselves through its language, words used to describe us and our behaviors, and the reward or punishment of different behaviors. Researchers currently believe that personality is at least partly innate and that it has significant bearing on both self-concept and communication.

Self-fulfilling prophecies derive from our own stated expectations of ourselves and those of others directed at us. Thus, if others say you are incompetent in some area (computer graphics) and act as if you are (assigning those tasks to others), you may be incompetent because you believe you are, and then you and others act in ways that make that true. On the other hand, if your boss sends you to training and assigns you computer graphic tasks, you may come to believe you are competent and, in fact, become competent. Self-fulfilling prophecies are powerful predictors of behavior and impact our communication with others and ourselves.

The way we frame our experiences, particularly experiences with others, creates the stories we tell ourselves, our narratives. If your sister-in-law does not invite you to a party, you might create a narrative of yourself as being snubbed by that side of the family. If you bring it to her attention with a perception check and find out she made an oversight or threw a party only for relatives with little kids, you can create a different, more accurate shared narrative together.

As the above example shows, sometimes our narratives are wrong; other times our understandings are distorted by common perceptual tendencies such as these:

- We judge ourselves with greater compassion and understanding than we judge others.

- We pay more attention to obvious stimuli such as motives, intensity, repetition, and contrast and pay less attention to more important factors.

- We cling to our first impressions even when they're wrong.

- We assume others are similar to us in their motives, needs and desires.

- Given competing impressions, we favor the negative ones.

- We blame innocent victims for what happens to them.

Cultural norms and rules influence what we "see" and how we view things; we tend to see events through the eyes of the culture embedded in us. For example, in a culture of individualism, pointing out your own strengths can help others view you as competent. In a collectivist culture, the same behavior could be labeled inappropriate, unconcerned with the group, and uncaring. Our capacity for empathy has an effect on our perceptions as well.

Using a perception check helps correct false perceptions and leads to better understanding of others. This skill consists of using nondefensive nonverbal behavior while stating to another the behavior you observed, proffering two possible interpretations, and requesting feedback from the other so that you can understand his or her behavior. While the perception check won't always bring understanding, its use goes far in preventing or correcting misunderstandings about others.

Chapter 2 Key Terms

For each of these terms, define the term, give an example, and explain the significance of the term.

1. empathy

2. face

3. facework

4. impression management

5. narratives

6. perceived self

7. perception checking

8. personality

9. presenting self

10. reflected appraisal

11. self-concept

12. self-esteem

13. self-fulfilling prophecy

14. self-serving bias

15. significant others

16. sympathy

Chapter 2 Review Questions

These questions are designed to help you understand this chapter's concepts and express your understanding in your own words. For practice with true/false and multiple-choice questions, use the CD-ROM you received with the text.

1. How do perceptual tendencies influence perception and lead to distortion?

2. How does culture impact both the perception and self-concept?

3. Why is empathy important in communication?

4. Identify ways in which you shape others' self-concepts and they shape yours.

5. How do both types of self-fulfilling prophecies affect communication and behavior?

6. Using your own examples, describe how your identity management process works to create various identities.

7. What are the ethical considerations of identity management?

8. Give an example of a situation in which you would be wise to use a perception check for greater accuracy. Write the perception check and label the parts.

Chapter 2 Thinking Outside the Box: Synthesizing Your Knowledge

These questions are designed to help you develop the big picture by blending what you've learned in this chapter and elsewhere.

1. How do characteristics of competent communicators (Chapter 1) coincide with perceptual concepts presented in this chapter?

2. How is Chapter 1's discussion of a transactional model related to this chapter's portrayal of self-concept?

Chapter 2 Answers to Review Questions

1. How do perceptual tendencies influence perception and lead to distortion?

    Judging others more harshly than we judge ourselves leads to distorted thinking—thinking that we are better than others or excusing our own behavior while believing others with the same behavior were acting rudely or wrongfully. When we use only information that is most obvious to us (such as intense, repetitious, or contrasting data or our own motives) to make sense of others' behaviors, we hold distorted views because we ignore factors that are less important. We seriously distort another person's behavior when we only "see" and believe that which reinforces a first impression. When we assume that others are similar to us, we believe we understand their needs, desires, and reactions, but we are simply reacting to our own. Favoring negative impressions over positive ones results in one-sided views of others rather than fair and balanced views. Finally, blaming victims for what happens to them leads to distorted views of people and situations, resulting in little understanding and much unwarranted criticism.

2. How does culture impact both the perception and self-concept?

    Everything we see, we see through the eyes of our own culture. The values we learned (primacy of the group or the individual, importance of talk or silence, value of time, money, and family) shape or filter all that we see. Cultures tell us what is valued in a person, so one's self-concept, particularly one's self-esteem, is shaped by the culture. A person who is direct and abrupt in a culture where those traits are valued will likely have higher self-esteem than the same person would in a culture where those traits are shunned. A culture's use of language to name and describe people impacts their self-concepts.

3. Why is empathy important in communication?

    The ability to step into another person's perspective and feel what the other person feels increases your ability to choose channels for communication effectiveness. If you empathize with another, you won't be shaking your head and wondering how they're feeling or how they could say or do something; instead, you'll have some insight into their reasons, feelings, and thoughts. When you empathize, you better understand the world from another's perspective and consequently better communicate with them.

4. Identify ways in which you shape others' self-concepts and they shape yours.

    Giving messages to others that say they are or are not competent, likeable, or deserving of respect shapes their opinions of themselves, particularly if this reflected appraisal is given to those for whom you are a significant other. If I repeatedly tell others by my words or actions that they either are or are not worthy of my time and attention, I mold their opinions of themselves. Conversely, if a person doesn't have time for me or constantly tells me that I can't do something or be something, this impacts my view of myself.

5. How do both types of self-fulfilling prophecies affect communication and behavior?

    If I repeatedly tell myself that I am or am not capable of doing something, then soon I believe it and act as if it's true, and it often becomes true. For instance, if I tell myself that I can learn ice hockey, and I sign up for training, join a team, and really work at it, I may do what I tell myself I can. This is a self-imposed self-fulfilling prophecy. If a parent or teacher tells me that I'll never manage fifteen credit hours and tells me I'll fail if I take a full load, I may begin to believe it and shape my behavior according to their words by giving up at midterm or not signing up for fifteen credit hours. Thus, I make their prediction or prophecy come true. Either way, these messages can be self-fulfilling prophecies that shape my self-concept and my behavior.

6. Using your own examples, describe how your identity management process works to create various identities.

    Responses will vary greatly with your identities. If you work in a particular career field (health, business, retail), you might describe the clothing (uniform), language, and behaviors that you use in that role. You might also have a particular role or identity in your family (oldest child, scholar, sports person) and describe how you act with family members. You will probably describe your identity in this classroom and how you shape it to influence your instructor and classmates so they view you in a particular way.

7. What are the ethical considerations of identity management?

    It is important to consider whether your portrayals of yourself are honest or dishonest. If you, in fact, are a hard worker, it is honest to try and persuade the interviewers that you will be a competent employee. However, to try and make others believe you really care about them and will be there if they have problems with the product you're selling them (when you know you won't) would be unethical behavior. You need to ask whether behavior is honest, good, and correct and causes no harm.

8. Give an example of a situation in which you would be wise to use a perception check for greater accuracy. Write the perception check and label the parts.

    You will probably think of many personal and professional situations in which you want to understand someone else. An example would be an instructor who tells you, "I think this course will be a challenge for you." You might use a perception check like this: "When you say this class will be a challenge for me (description of behavior), I wonder if you mean that I should drop the course (one interpretation) or if you mean that it will be tough but I'll make it and have a lot of my beliefs challenged (second interpretation). Could you give me a better idea of what you mean?" (request for feedback)

Chapter 2 Answers to Thinking Outside the Box

1. How do characteristics of competent communicators (Chapter 1) coincide with perceptual concepts presented in this chapter?

   Three of the characteristics of a competent communicator discussed in Chapter 1 are empathy, cognitive complexity, and self-monitoring. These three traits correlate closely with this chapter's discussion of empathy and how it combines the ability to take another's cognitive and emotional perspective in order to better perceive another. So cognitive complexity and empathy are important to understanding someone's thoughts and feelings, which is to say their perception of things.

   Self-monitoring requires an awareness of one's self-concept and the perceptual factors that are influencing you. It requires an honest look at oneself to see how one's self-concept and self-esteem are affecting perception.

2. How is Chapter 1's discussion of a transactional model related to this chapter's portrayal of self-concept?

   *The **transactional model** shows that each person simultaneously **encodes** and **decodes** messages. What we know from the study of self-concept is that it simultaneously affects both processes. We send messages that match our self-concepts. If someone believes she is a competent leader, she is more apt to communicate that by stepping up and taking a leadership role in a group. If one's self-concept does not include characteristics of leadership, he may hear (decode) someone's suggestion that he take a leadership role with fear rather than satisfaction and pride. On the other hand, such a message from a significant other may shape his self-concept and lead him to believe that he can be a leader. In either case, the self-concept influences what messages we send to others and how messages that are sent by others are decoded. [Boldfaced words are from Chapter 1.]*

CHAPTER 3 LANGUAGE

SQ3R in Action

Generate an SQ3R chart for this chapter here: www.teach-nology.com/web_tools/ graphic_org/sq3r/

Survey

Skim the title, Chapter Highlights, objectives ("You should understand" and "You should be able to"), headings, tables, photos, cartoons, figures, charts, and items in the margin. Glance at the titles of the Critical Thinking Probes and Ethical Challenges. At the end of each chapter, look over the list of Key Terms, Activities, and Resources.

Question

Ask yourself questions. What do you know about these topics from your own life experiences and from other classes? Ask these six questions in each section: who, what, when, where, how, and why.

Read

Take one heading at a time and read to find the answers to the questions you've posed.

Recite

In your own words, say the answer aloud and then write it out.

Review

Review each section and then review the whole chapter. This is a good time to use the activities at the end of each chapter and the activities and the sample exams on the CD-ROM. Remember to periodically review the previous chapters as well.

Chapter 3 Outline

(Italicized words are key terms.)

I. Understanding symbols, meanings, and rules is essential to understanding *language's* important characteristics.
   A. Language is symbolic; it is constructed with *symbols.*
   B. Meanings are in people, not in words.
   C. Language is governed by *phonological, syntactic, semantic,* and *pragmatic rules.*
II. Language has the power to shape and reflect attitudes.
   A. The use of language in naming people and groups, establishing credibility,

instituting status, and increasing or diminishing sexism and racism demonstrates the power of language to shape attitudes.

    B. Language reflects attitudes, as we use it to demonstrate our power, affiliation (through *convergence* or *divergence*), attraction and interest (through demonstrative pronouns, negation, or sequential placement), and responsibility (through the use of "I" language, "but," and questions).

III. Troublesome language leads to misunderstandings, disruptions, and evasions.

    A. *Equivocal words, relative words, slang, jargon, abstract language,* and stereotyping lead to misunderstandings; behavioral descriptions reduce these confusions.

    B. Using *emotive language* and failing to differentiate between *factual statements, opinion statements,* and *inferential statements* lead to disruption and confusion in communication.

    C. *Euphemisms* and *equivocations* are types of evasive language that avoid completely truthful statements.

IV. Gender differences influence our language use.

    A. The content of language used by men and women demonstrates gender differences.

    B. Motives and reasons for communicating differ with gender.

    C. Conversational style differs with gender.

    D. Some differences in communication between genders are a result of social philosophy, occupations, and social and *sex roles* rather than gender.

V. Culture and language are interdependent; *low-* and *high-context cultures* illustrate this interdependence.

    A. Languages exhibit diverse cultural styles with regard to directness/indirectness, elaborateness/succinctness, and formality/informality.

    B. The *Whorf-Sapir hypothesis* and the discussion of *linguistic determinism* or *relativism* illustrate how language shapes our worldviews.

    C. Surnames and ethnic names shape and reflect attitudes in North American culture.

Chapter 3 Summary

Language can facilitate or interfere with effective communication. This chapter highlights the fundamental characteristics of language, ways that language both shapes and reflects our attitudes, problems caused by certain types of language, gender and cultural factors, and the correlation between language, culture, and worldview.

First, a fundamental characteristic of language is that it is symbolic; arbitrarily chosen symbols (words) represent things but are not those things. We often react to the symbols rather than to the actual person or thing. Second, meanings don't exist in the words but in the person saying, hearing, or seeing them. Third, language is governed by rules: phonological rules about the sounds of words, semantic rules about the meanings of words, syntactic rules about the order of words, and pragmatic rules about the practical use of words.

It is possible to see how the language used to describe people and experiences shapes our attitudes, feelings, and thoughts toward a person, group, or event. If you learned to call police officers by that name rather than a derogatory name, the language you use shapes your attitude. If you learned respectful language to refer to people of other cultures, those words mold your attitude toward other cultures. The language you use enhances or lessens your credibility and status in the eyes of others. Language can increase or decrease sexism and racism in individuals and groups; for instance, if sexist or racist terms are constantly used in a particular workplace or home, the climate is different from a context where such language is never used.

The language we choose reflects our attitudes. Our words signal to others whether we believe our power is less than, equal to, or greater than theirs. Our language choices tell others whether we are trying to join with them or be distant from them (convergence or divergence). We clue others about our attraction and interest to them or to things through demonstrative pronouns, negation, and sequential placement. For instance, saying "we" or "us" rather than "they" or "them" signals a cohesiveness or similarity rather than divisiveness or difference. Using "I" language, rather than "you" or "it" language, takes responsibility for one's own thoughts, feelings, and wants, as in "I feel humiliated" rather than "You make me feel humiliated." Questions (Do you want to go eat?) also avoid responsibility for one's needs (I'd like to go eat.). Using "but" often negates everything that came before it, as in "I'd like to hire her, but she doesn't finish projects."

Some types of language disrupt, bewilder, and evade. Equivocal words have more than one commonly used and perfectly acceptable definition. When context doesn't clearly signal which meaning is intended, serious misunderstandings occur and may damage relationships. A faculty member told a student that a particular book might help her and told her to "check it out," meaning to peruse it. The student literally checked out the book from the library, although it was of no help, and then felt embarrassed at her misunderstanding. Relative words cause confusion by not stating numerically or comparatively what is intended; telling someone to wait "a bit" could mean an hour or only a few minutes. Slang and jargon are used by certain groups (cocultural, professional, students) and not always widely understood by others outside that group. Adjusting your vocabulary to your conversationalists is wise. Abstract language is vague and general and avoids details about what is referred to. This leads to stereotyping and confusion. Behavioral descriptions lesson confusion because they move down the abstraction ladder and give specific information about who and what. ("My son who is in the First Infantry Division in Iraq" is more specific than the abstract word "soldier.") Euphemisms and equivocations may avoid unpleasant topics or be deliberate lies. To say you "misrepresented" something when you know you lied is to use a euphemism to deceive.

"Right-sizing" to mean firing 20 percent of employees may be a euphemism to make something nasty sound better.

Although men and women speak the same language, their speech varies in content, use, and conversational style. Researchers have discovered that some patterns of speech are more characteristic of men and some are more characteristic of women. None of the research claims that all men or all women follow these patterns, nor that men's and women's patterns aren't changing. Still, men and women tend to speak about different topics in same-sex conversations and use language for different purposes. Women build relationships and meet social needs through language, while men use language to accomplish tasks and assert their power, status, and independence. Conversational styles vary: men use more statements and interruptions while women use more questions and intensifiers. However, not all differences between men and women are due to gender, because occupational and social roles and social philosophy impact language use, too.

Language is a significant part of any culture, and language and culture shape each other. Cultures carry deep-seated beliefs about how and when to use language. Low-context cultures use and expect a lot of direct talk, whereas high-context cultures value silence, observation, and less direct speech. Some cultures use more elaborate language, while others are far more succinct. Yet another variable reflected in the language is the level of formality expressed in and expected as part of the culture.

The language people speak actually shapes their perceptions of the world and its events. Cultures develop words for what is important in that culture. English has many words for computers, their parts, and functions. The words then influence how people see and discuss events. For instance, if someone forgets something, they might use an expression relating their memory to their hard drive. Whether a language emphasizes "having" or "doing" reflects cultural ideas and then influences perceptions of events. The theory of linguistic relativism emphasizes language's influence on perceptions, so concepts that are nonexistent in a culture have no words to express the concept in their language.

Language is a complex and culturally interdependent set of symbols that can create understanding among people or cause divisive distortions. Knowledge of language and its characteristics and skills in using language increase the chances of understanding others and being understood by them.

Chapter 3 Key Terms

For each of these terms, define the term, give an example, and explain the significance of the term.

1. abstract language

2. abstraction ladder

3. behavioral description

4. convergence

5. divergence

6. emotive language

7. equivocal words

8. equivocation

9. euphemism

10. factual statement

11. high-context culture

12. inferential statement

13. jargon

14. language

15. linguistic determinism

16. linguistic relativism

17. low-context culture

18. opinion statement

19. phonological rules

20. pragmatic rules

21. relative rules

22. semantic rules

23. sex role

24. slang

25. symbols

26. syntactic rules

27. Whorf-Sapir hypothesis

Chapter 3 Review Questions

These questions are designed to help you understand this chapter's concepts and express your understanding in your own words. For practice with true/false and multiple-choice questions, use the CD-ROM you received with the text.

1. What does the statement that "language is symbolic and person-centered" mean?

2. Describe how four different types of rules affect language use.

3. Explain with examples how language both shapes and reflects attitudes.

4. Explain four types of troublesome language and what skills can be used to lessen the detrimental impact of each type. Choose from equivocal words, slang and jargon, relative terms, overly abstract language, and euphemisms.

5. What are some key differences in the way men and women use language?

6. What is the correlation between one's culture (worldview) and language?

Chapter 3 Thinking Outside the Box: Synthesizing Your Knowledge

These questions are designed to help you develop the big picture by blending what you've learned in this chapter and elsewhere.

1. How might a person's use of language be related to his or her self-concept? How does language contribute to create a self-fulfilling prophecy? (Chapter 2)

2. How is language used in identity management? (Chapter 2)

Chapter 3 Answers to Review Questions

1. What does the statement that "language is symbolic and person-centered" mean?

Language consists of arbitrary symbols (words) designated to represent something. There is no reason why "table" is used in English and "mesa" in Spanish. These are arbitrary. Language is also person-centered because the meaning of words does not come from the words themselves but from the associations and experiences one has had with the word. Each person brings his or her own meanings of words to a conversation, so we try to find common ground and negotiate shared meanings, all the while remembering that meanings are personally created.

2. Describe how four different types of rules affect language use.

Phonological rules govern the way sounds are put together in different languages. For instance, words that begin with the consonants "ts" are uncommon in words of English origin; most words beginning with "ts" have Japanese (tsunami), Russian (tsar), or other origins. Syntactic rules govern the sequence of words, so English speakers say "white shirt," with the adjective before the noun, while in Spanish speakers say the equivalent of "shirt white," with the noun before the adjective. Semantic rules govern the meanings of words, and it is generally agreed-upon meanings that allow us to communicate with words at all. Pragmatic rules deal with the way language is used in everyday situations. For instance, if someone asks,

"Do you have the time?" the pragmatic rule is that if you have it, you give the time. You don't just answer "yes," although it is syntactically a yes/no question. It is these pragmatic rules that require knowledge of the context and culture.

3. Explain with examples how language both shapes and reflects attitudes.

    We use words to describe the world as we see it, and the words we use often reflect our attitudes. Whether a parent uses the term "high achiever" or "apple polisher" to refer to a child who strives for all As reflects the parent's attitude toward the behavior. Those words then shape the attitude of the child and her siblings. A teacher who commends a student for being "assertive" for insisting on her place in line shapes different attitudes in her students than a teacher who labels the same behavior as "rude." In each case, the language reflects attitudes of the speaker and then shapes attitudes of others.

4. Explain four types of troublesome language and what skills can be used to lessen the detrimental impact of each type. Choose from equivocal words, slang and jargon, relative terms, overly abstract language, and euphemisms.

    Equivocal words have two very different meanings, and confusion occurs when two people interpret a word differently. John's car is "hot" could mean overheated, stolen, 100 degrees, or very nice. When using an equivocal word, you might pair it with another one that clarifies your meaning. Slang and jargon are words used by a particular group of people and not widely understood outside that group. When speaking to people outside your group (culture, profession, or region), eliminate the slang and jargon. Relative terms are widely misunderstood because "big" and "small" or "long" and "short" have different meanings for each of us. Rather than use relative words, use numerical words: "twenty pounds," "four pages," or "six o'clock." Overly abstract words are vague and too general. Replace them with concrete, specific words and with behavioral descriptions. Rather than saying "college students," clarify which students you are talking about: "Students who took Communication with me last year." Speakers use euphemisms and equivocations to avoid what is true or unpleasant; description and more-accurate language reduce confusion.

5. What are some key differences in the way men and women use language?

    Men and women use language to talk about different things (content), for different purposes, and in different styles. Men's conversations focus more on current events, sports, and business, while women's conversations focus more on family and relationships. Men and women seem to have different goals for conversations. Men often use conversations to accomplish a task, to affirm their status, or to maintain independence. Women often use conversation to build connections and create harmony and to reduce status or power. For these reasons, men and women view checking with a spouse before making plans differently. Men see it as a lack of independence, whereas women see it as sustaining connection. Men's and women's conversational styles vary because women make greater efforts to sustain conversation and use more questions and intensifiers and less powerful speech. Men use more declarative statements, directives, indicators of status, and interruptions.

6.   What is the correlation between one's culture (worldview) and language?

Language and culture are so intertwined that one of the key characteristics of any culture is its language. A language both reflects and reinforces what is important in a given culture because there will be words for that which is important. The Japanese have a word "ōn," which refers to an obligation you owe that can never be repaid to the person to whom it is owed, such as that to your parents or to a teacher. English has no equivalent word or translation because that concept is not a significant one. Thus, language and culture reinforce each other, and the way you see the world is shaped by the words you have to describe that world.

Chapter 3 Answers to Thinking Outside the Box

1.   How might a person's use of language be related to his or her self-concept? How does language contribute to create a self-fulfilling prophecy? (Chapter 2)

*If parents or other **significant others** use particular words to refer to a child, that child hears that language as **reflected appraisal** and molds those words into his or her self-concept. Parents who refer to their children as "gifted" or "athletic" and put them in such programs, help create that self-concept in the child. Parents who repeatedly refer to a child as a loser or underachiever can instill that image in the child, also. If the child takes that language (label) to heart and believes it and acts as if it is true, it can indeed become a **self-fulfilling prophecy**. [Boldfaced words are from Chapter 2.]*

2.   How is language used in identity management? (Chapter 2)

*Because language can both reflect and shape one's identity, it is a key factor in **impression management**. The kind of language we use to refer to and describe ourselves to others helps us create the identity we want. For instance, a woman who wants to be seen as more independent may refer to herself as "Ms." rather than "Miss" or "Mrs." She may use her own family name rather than her husband's name. A doctor who wants to be recognized as such even among friends might prefer being called "Doc" to a first name. Someone who sells makeup might prefer to be called a cosmetic consultant rather than a makeup salesperson. In many ways, the language we use to refer to ourselves shapes our identity in the eyes of others. [Boldfaced words are from Chapter 2.]*

CHAPTER 4 LISTENING

SQ3R in Action

Generate an SQ3R chart for this chapter here: www.teach-nology.com/web_tools/ graphic_org/sq3r/

Survey

Skim the title, Chapter Highlights, objectives ("You should understand" and "You should be able to"), headings, tables, photos, cartoons, figures, charts, and items in the margin. Glance at the titles of the Critical Thinking Probes and Ethical Challenges. At the end of each chapter, look over the list of Key Terms, Activities, and Resources.

Question

Ask yourself questions. What do you know about these topics from your own life experiences and from other classes? Ask these six questions in each section: who, what, when, where, how, and why.

Read

Take one heading at a time and read to find the answers to the questions you've posed.

Recite

In your own words, say the answer aloud and then write it out.

Review

Review each section and then review the whole chapter. This is a good time to use the activities at the end of each chapter and the activities and the sample exams on the CD-ROM. Remember to periodically review the previous chapters as well.

Chapter 4 Outline

(Italicized words are key terms.)

I. Replacing misconceptions about *listening* with accurate beliefs can improve listening.
    A. Hearing is a physiological process; listening is psychological and involves *attending, understanding, responding,* and *remembering* (the *residual message*).
    B. Listening is not a natural process, but one that we can improve on.
    C. Listening requires a great deal of effort to do well.
    D. Listeners have different interpretations while hearing the same message.

II. To improve listening, try to understand the many types of faulty listening and overcome various barriers to listening.
   A. Improve listening by avoiding these faulty listening behaviors: *pseudolistening, selective listening, defensive listening, ambushing, insulated listening, insensitive listening,* and *stage hogging.*
   B. Improve listening by eliminating or minimizing these barriers: lack of effort, message overload, rapid thought, psychological noise, physical noise, hearing problems, faulty assumptions, apparent advantages of talking, cultural differences, and media influences.
III. Identify and be aware of your own and others' personal listening styles.
   A. *Content-oriented listeners* pay careful attention to the particulars and the specific details.
   B. *People-oriented listeners* focus on the speaker's emotional state and relational issues.
   C. *Action-oriented listeners* center their listening on the mission and listen to better achieve a goal.
   D. *Time-oriented listeners* are conscious of how long the conversation is taking and may be distracted or anxious with lengthy speakers.
IV. *Informational listening* requires effort and strategy.
   A. Don't argue with the speaker or judge remarks prematurely.
   B. Listen to the message even if you dislike the speaker.
   C. Take the opportunity to learn from all speakers, whether skilled or not.
   D. Listen for key ideas, not minute details or tangential remarks.
   E. Ask sincere questions, not counterfeit questions.
   F. Paraphrase the speaker by putting thoughts and feelings into your own words.
   G. Record key ideas by developing and using a note-taking technique.
V. *Critical* (evaluative) *listening* requires you to listen and evaluate what you hear.
   A. Listen for complete information before evaluating the speaker.
   B. Assess the speaker's credibility, including competence and impartiality.
   C. Examine the speaker's evidence and reasoning by considering whether evidence is recent, thorough, and valid.
   D. Examine and think critically about the speaker's emotional appeals.
VI. *Empathic listening* requires considerable discernment and skill.
   A. *Advising* others is risky because it isn't always clear whether others want advice, and you may or may not have the best advice.
   B. Before using *judging* responses, consider whether your judgment was requested and whether it is constructive in the context.
   C. *Analyzing* is precarious, unless you're tentative, reasonably correct, well motivated, and sure the speaker is receptive to your analysis.
   D. *Questioning* responses are best if questions are not distracting and not used to disguise suggestions or criticism—in other words, you're sure your questions

are *sincere questions* rather than *counterfeit questions*.
E. *Supporting* responses require your sincerity and the other's acceptance.
F. *Prompting* uses minimal responses to encourage the other to speak.
G. *Paraphrasing* a speaker's thoughts and feelings helps him or her clarify potentially troublesome thoughts and feelings.
　　1. Successful paraphrasing depends on whether you have adequate time, concern, and ability to express interest in a nonjudgmental way.
　　2. Consider whether helping responses are appropriate for this situation, this person, and your own abilities and limitations.

Chapter 4 Summary

Listening is a vital element of communication, but listening is not just one skill or one behavior; it is a complex set of skills and behaviors that vary with the situation. Listening competence requires a variety of skills and the ability to know which ones to use when.

Informational listening is the method to use to understand another. It requires an ability to withhold judgment rather than rush to judgment, to ask sincere questions, to paraphrase thoughts and feelings, and to take notes accurately. It also calls for the capability to summarize key ideas rather than get bogged down in details, and it requires an attitude of "I can learn," whether listening to a skilled or unskilled speaker. The informational listener pays close attention to the speaker without being distracted by personal biases or by annoying habits of the speaker. Paraphrasing accurately challenges the listener to be attentive to what is said in order to make an accurate guess at the speaker's thoughts and feelings without sounding judgmental or creating defensiveness in the speaker.

Critical listening is not listening to criticize in a negative sense; its goal is determining the legitimacy or worth of the message, so it is vital in personal and professional encounters. Although the ultimate purpose of critical listening is to judge the validity of information, doing this well requires the listener to first withhold judgment and understand and process complete information. The listener must analyze the speaker's data and reasoning by asking if the support presented is recent, thorough, reliable, and correctly interpreted. The listener must also sort through a speaker's emotional appeals.

A third type of listening and responding, empathic listening, is useful to build relationships and help others by thoughtfully understanding another's point of view. Advising, judging, analyzing, questioning, supporting, prompting, and paraphrasing can be used empathically to help others. These seemingly diverse empathic response styles must be used with caution; in trying to be empathic and helpful, caution is needed so that the listener is not perceived as threatening or invasive. Used poorly, they damage relationships and are not helpful. In each situation, the listener must carefully consider the whole context, the other person's particular perceptions, needs, and personality, and the listener's relationships, abilities, and perceptions.

This chapter introduces four personal listening styles. Content-oriented listeners pay careful attention to the details and facts of what is said. People-oriented listeners are most attentive to the speaker's feelings and overall well-being. Action-oriented listeners focus on the mission and listen for ways to accomplish a goal. Time-oriented listeners are most aware of the clock and the minutes ticking away. Knowing your style and the style of people you are listening to helps you analyze and improve listening situations.

To be more effective at all types of listening, minimize problem listening behaviors and understand and curtail reasons for poor listening. The behaviors that undermine successful communication include pretending to listening (pseudolistening), listening only for what you want to hear (selective listening), listening as if you are under attack (defensive listening), listening to be able to attack others (ambushing), avoiding topics (insulated listening), not paying attention to feelings or hidden meanings (insensitive listening), or listening only to call attention to oneself (stage hogging). Understand, manage, or eliminate these barriers to listening: lack of effort; too many messages; rapid thought; physical, physiological, and psychological noise; false assumptions; perceived advantages of talking rather than listening; and cultural and media influences.

Listening improves if we let go of mistaken beliefs about listening and replace them with facts. Hearing and listening are not the same; hearing is physiological while listening requires more mental and psychological involvement and requires effort. Listening doesn't come naturally, but it is a skill we can learn and improve. Communication is a transactional process in which listeners don't always receive the same message the speaker believes she is sending. Individuals interpret messages and hear them in many different ways

To summarize, listening is a skill that is complex and multifaceted and can always be improved. Communicating well requires awareness of and attention to our listening skills.

Chapter 4 Key Terms

For each of these terms, define the term, give an example, and explain the significance of the term.

1. action-oriented listeners

2. advising

3. ambushers

4. analyzing

5. attending

6. content-oriented listeners

7. counterfeit question

8. critical listening

9. defensive listening

10. empathic listening

11. hearing

12. informational listening

13. insensitive listeners

14. insulated listeners

15. judging

16. listening

17. paraphrasing

18. people-oriented listeners

19. prompting

20. pseudolistening

21. questioning

22. remembering

23. residual message

24. responding

25. selective listening

26. sincere question

27. stage hogs

28. supporting

29. time-oriented listeners

30. understanding

Chapter 4 Review Questions

These questions are designed to help you understand this chapter's concepts and express your understanding in your own words. For practice with true/false and multiple-choice questions, use the CD-ROM you received with the text.

1. In your own words, identify common misconceptions about listening.

2. Of the common types of ineffective listening, give examples of the three that affect you the most and describe the consequences.

3. For each of the four personal listening styles, describe a time when each listening style would be an advantage.

4. Rank-order the challenges that make effective listening difficult for you. Explain your rankings.

5. For each of the three major types of listening discussed in the chapter, what skills and attitudes are needed?

Chapter 4 Thinking Outside the Box: Synthesizing Your Knowledge

These questions are designed to help you develop the big picture by blending what you've learned in this chapter and elsewhere.

1. In Chapter 1, you learned about several characteristics of competent communicators. Which of these relate to listening?

2. Chapter 3 described abstract language. How might the concept of the abstraction ladder be useful in thinking about paraphrasing?

Chapter 4 Answers to Review Questions

1. In your own words, identify common misconceptions about listening.

   A. *Sometimes people think that listening and hearing are the same; in fact, we hear if the sound waves strike our eardrums. Listening requires mental alertness and attention. We can hear but not listen, proving the two are not the same.*

   B. *Some people think listening is natural, that we just do it. In fact, it is a skill that can be studied, practiced, and improved.*

   C. *People assume that listening is easy; in fact, it requires a lot of effort and energy.*

   D. *Another misconception is that if we speak, everyone hears what we say in the same way. Actually, each person perceives what is said based on his or her own experiences, beliefs, and needs, so each constructs, or "hears," a different version of what a person said.*

2. Of the common types of ineffective listening, give examples of the three that affect you the most and describe the consequences.

Answers will vary greatly, choosing from these types of ineffective listening: pseudolistening, ambushing, stage hogging, and selective, defensive, insulated, or insensitive listening. Sample consequences: If I am pseudolistening and someone asks me what they've just said, I am embarrassed that I didn't really listen, especially if it is a close friend. When I've been the stage hog, I often found out too late that the person I "hogged" from was someone I needed to listen to, could have learned from, or really hurt. When I listened defensively to an instructor who inquired into how I'd been taught to do a type of algebra problem, I started defending the way I'd been taught and thought I was being reprimanded. I missed an opportunity to learn a new way and also damaged my relationship with that instructor.

3. For each of the four personal listening styles, describe a time when each listening style would be an advantage.

    Content-oriented listeners are needed when one has to listen carefully to a lot of information and be able to analyze ideas and understand different approaches. They're valuable when one listens to sales pitches, realtors, or college recruiters, for example. People-oriented listeners are wonderful at the dinner table or when meeting new people because they center on relationships and care about the feelings of all. Action-oriented listeners are advantageous when working on a task, as they'll keep others focused on the work to be done. Time-oriented listeners are advantageous when it is imperative to watch the clock and meet a deadline.

4. Rank-order the challenges that make effective listening difficult for you. Explain your rankings.

    Answers will vary greatly. The challenges mentioned in the text include media influences, cultural differences, apparent advantages of talking rather than listening, faulty assumptions, hearing problems, physical noise, psychological noise, rapid thought, message overload, and effort.

5. For each of the three major types of listening discussed in the chapter, what skills and attitudes are needed?

    Informational listening requires an attitude of genuinely wanting to learn. The skills needed include the ability to suspend judgment, to summarize details into key ideas and broader concepts, and to take notes efficiently.

    Critical listening likewise requires the ability to suspend judgment and to evaluate the speaker's credibility, evidence, reasoning, and emotional appeals. The critical listener needs to discern what is factual, valid, and authoritative.

    Empathic listening requires the listener to carefully determine what type of response is appropriate. Advising, judging, analyzing, questioning, supporting, prompting, and paraphrasing can all be used empathically, but each carries risks to the relationship. An attitude of openness and awareness of these risks is important. The listener needs to have a cautious attitude and be alert for signs of defensiveness when trying to listen empathically.

Chapter 4 Answers to Thinking Outside the Box

1. In Chapter 1, you learned about several characteristics of competent communicators. Which of these relate to listening?

    __Communication competence__ necessitates choosing the most appropriate behavior for the situation. This requires competent listening to know what the situation is and to evaluate it accurately. One must listen to understand the communication __environment__ and wisely choose the best approach. Eliminating __noise__ and understanding the __transactional__ nature of communication enhances the ability to listen. Another characteristic of competent communicators is the ability to skillfully enact a chosen behavior. If the most appropriate behavior is listening, then all of the listening skills contribute to communication competence. Another skill discussed in Chapter 1, demonstrating empathy, requires careful listening to understand another's thoughts and feelings. Cognitive complexity, which involves understanding another person's perspective, is possible with careful listening. [Boldfaced words are from Chapter 1.]

2. Chapter 3 described abstract language. How might the concept of the abstraction ladder be useful in thinking about paraphrasing?

    The __abstraction ladder__ is a useful tool to think of ways to paraphrase someone else. If the person gives you details, "You know what happened today? First my computer crashed, then my business instructor gave me added assignments. I didn't get lunch at all, and the copier broke in the middle of my project that's due tomorrow," you might paraphrase up the abstraction ladder by summarizing more generally what was said, "Sounds like you're overwhelmed with what you need to accomplish." If a speaker uses __abstract, equivocal,__ or __relative language__, you might paraphrase down the abstraction ladder to try to find out what's going on: "That instructor gives too much work. I just hate it." You could paraphrase, "You have to complete an exam or paper every week?" [Boldfaced words are from Chapter 3.]

CHAPTER 5 NONVERBAL COMMUNICATION

SQ3R in Action

Generate an SQ3R chart for this chapter here: www.teach-nology.com/web_tools/graphic_org/sq3r/

Survey

Skim the title, Chapter Highlights, objectives ("You should understand" and "You should be able to"), headings, tables, photos, cartoons, figures, charts, and items in the margin. Glance at the titles of the Critical Thinking Probes and Ethical Challenges. At the end of each chapter, look over the list of Key Terms, Activities, and Resources.

Question

Ask yourself questions. What do you know about these topics from your own life experiences and from other classes? Ask these six questions in each section: who, what, when, where, how, and why.

Read

Take one heading at a time and read to find the answers to the questions you've posed.

Recite

In your own words, say the answer aloud and then write it out.

Review

Review each section and then review the whole chapter. This is a good time to use the activities at the end of each chapter and the activities and the sample exams on the CD-ROM. Remember to periodically review the previous chapters as well.

Chapter 5 Outline

(Italicized words are key terms.)

I. Effective communication requires an understanding of the fundamental characteristics of *nonverbal communication.*

    A. Nonverbal communication always exists in face-to-face communication, and some elements exist in interpersonal relationships, even when people aren't physically present with each other.

    B. Nonverbal behavior—whether intentional or unintentional, conscious or unconscious—does communicate to others.

    C. Nonverbal communication expresses many dimensions of relationships; it serves to manage identity, define relationships, and express attitudes and emotions.

D. Nonverbal communication is even more ambiguous than verbal communication, so it is important to consider the context, relational history, and feelings of all persons involved.

II. Culture and gender shape the way we decode and encode nonverbal communication.

A. Gestures, distances, and eye contact vary in different cultures.

B. Biology, social factors, status, and culture all impact nonverbal gender differences.

III. Nonverbal communication serves one or more functions in relationship to verbal communication.

A. Nonverbal communication **repeats** what is said verbally.

B. Nonverbal communication **substitutes** for words.

C. Nonverbal behaviors **complement** what is said verbally, often by using *illustrators.*

D. Nonverbal communication **accents** spoken words.

E. Nonverbal communication **regulates** behaviors and conversations.

F. When nonverbal communication gives the opposite message of the verbal communication, it **contradicts** the verbal message.

G. Nonverbal communication may be used to **deceive others**.

IV. Communicators use various types of nonverbal communication to express themselves.

A. *Kinesics* (the study of body movement) includes messages conveyed through posture and gestures and includes the use of *manipulators* and *emblems.*

B. Our faces and eyes communicate emotional and relational messages, sometimes with *affect blends.*

C. Our voices *(paralanguage)* impart messages through tone, speed, pitch, volume, and pauses and *disfluencies.*

D. Touch, a necessary early form of communication, conveys messages about the type of relationship that exists.

E. Physical attractiveness influences personal and professional communication throughout life.

F. Clothing is most important in early stages of relationships, signaling status and influencing interactions.

G. *Proxemics* (the study of the use of space) classifies the distances at which we communicate: *intimate, personal, social,* or *public.*

H. Time *(chronemics)* communicates status and cultural concepts.

I. Power and status are often communicated by claiming and using *territory.*

J. Environments provide valuable information to communicators that shape impressions and interactions.

Chapter 5 Summary

Nonverbal communication adds complexity to the process of communication in part because nonverbal communication never ceases. The many types and functions of nonverbal communication and the influences of culture and gender add other layers of complexity to the process.

Underpinning all nonverbal communication are some basic principles: nonverbal communication always exists in face-to-face communication and in much communication that is not face-to-face. Nonverbal behaviors, whether intentional or unintentional, communicate a great deal about each of us. Nonverbal communication contains multiple layers of meaning with regard to feelings, attitudes, and relational messages. Additionally, nonverbal communication is far more ambiguous than verbal communication.

Nonverbal communication performs many functions. It is easy to imagine a communicator consciously holding up two fingers to repeat the spoken word "two" or to substitute the nonverbal for the verbal by holding up two fingers without speaking. Like expressive storytellers, many people "talk with their hands," accenting and complementing their words with facial and eye expressions, movements, and gestures. People use eye contact, head nods, and smiles to regulate conversations and let others know when to talk and when to refrain from speaking. Instructors regulate side conversations with proxemics and kinesics by walking near talkative students. Nonverbal behavior sometimes functions to contradict the verbal message, consciously or unconsciously. Still other times, nonverbal communication may be used to consciously deceive someone.

Because communication is multichanneled, many types of nonverbal communication occur simultaneously. These include posture, gestures, face and eye behavior, voice, touch, physical appearance, distance, time, territoriality, and the physical environment itself. It is easy to imagine one communication situation in which the physical environment (classroom) sends messages about how to behave while at the same time regulating the distance at which students and teacher interact. Class has a designated time to begin, and students who violate that time expectation are designated as "tardy" and often seen as rude and disrespectful as well. Students demonstrate territoriality by sitting in the same seats each class, even when seats are not assigned. Each person's postures, gestures, facial expressions, eye contact, and physical appearance send continuous messages to others. Vocal characteristics such as volume, pitch, rate, and tone convey more information to classmates. Each person's physical appearance and dress influence whether interaction with others occurs and the nature of that interaction. Attractiveness as defined by the culture or coculture further shapes interactions.

Culture and gender make a difference in people's perception of and enactment of nonverbal communication. Each culture attaches distinct meanings to gestures, defines appropriate interactional distances, and follows clear rules with regard to eye contact (when, where, with whom, and how much). The meanings and rules vary from culture to culture, so lack of eye contact may signal respect in one culture and disrespect or deceit in another. Gender differences in nonverbal communication result from differences in biology, size, social factors, status, and culture, so that a behavior by a man may have a very different meaning and impact than that same behavior by a woman.

To sum up, because nonverbal communication is ambiguous, communicators need be aware of the present context (when, where, and with whom one is communicating), the history of a relationship, and the current moods and feelings of all involved. Nonverbal communication serves many functions and happens in many channels concurrently. We are continuously and simultaneously sending and receiving, encoding and decoding a multitude of nonverbal messages.

Chapter 5 Key Terms

For each of these terms, define the term, give an example, and explain the significance of the term.

1. affect blends

2. chronemics

3. disfluencies

4. emblems

5. illustrators

6. intimate distance

7. kinesics

8. manipulators

9. nonverbal communication

10. paralanguage

11. personal distance

12. proxemics

13. public distance

14. social distance

15. territory

Chapter 5 Review Questions

These questions are designed to help you understand this chapter's concepts and express your understanding in your own words. For practice with true/false and multiple-choice questions, use the CD-ROM you received with the text.

What are four key characteristics of nonverbal communication?

How do culture and gender influence nonverbal communication?

List seven functions of nonverbal communication and give an example of each.

Describe ten types of nonverbal communication and an example of how each is commonly used.

Describe important categories communicators use in describing distance and voice (proxemics and paralanguage).

Chapter 5 Thinking Outside the Box: Synthesizing Your Knowledge

These questions are designed to help you develop the big picture by blending what you've learned in this chapter and elsewhere.

Both language (Chapter 3) and nonverbal communication are described as ambiguous. Compare and contrast the reasons for each being labeled ambiguous.

How can perception checks (Chapter 2) help you to be a more effective nonverbal communicator?

Chapter 5 Answers to Review Questions

What are four key characteristics of nonverbal communication?

The four fundamental characteristics of nonverbal communication are 1) it always exists when communicating face-to-face, 2) you cannot avoid communicating nonverbally, 3) it is far more ambiguous than language, and 4) behavior always has the potential to be interpreted, whether intentional or not. Nonverbal communication conveys much information on a relational level; it defines, expresses, and shapes the relationship. Meanings vary with culture, gender, and a host of other factors.

How do culture and gender influence nonverbal communication?

Men and women learn different rules or norms for nonverbal communication and then are judged differently based on those rules. Women smile and gesture more than men; men interact at greater distances and take greater personal space. Rules regarding gestures, distance, and eye contact vary greatly among cultures around the world and among cocultures within a nation. Awareness of the different meanings attached to gestures and the appropriate distances and eye behavior for interacting with others will smooth intercultural interactions.

3. Describe seven functions of nonverbal communication and give an example of each.

Nonverbal communication serves many purposes. It can repeat what is said verbally such as telling someone "I love you" and then hugging the person. You can substitute a hug and use no words at all, letting action speak for itself. You might complement your words by showing with your hands the design you are describing verbally. You could accent your words with nonverbal behaviors such as using a louder voice to emphasize a word or syllable or clapping your hands to accent your joy. We use our voices and eye contact to let others know when we are done talking, when we want the floor, and when we want to continue talking, thereby regulating others' behavior. Mixed messages are sent when the verbal and nonverbal messages contradict each other, so saying "I'm sorry" in a sarcastic voice or saying "I hate you" with a smile and a twinkle in your eye will usually result in the nonverbal behavior being believed. Finally, sometimes nonverbal behavior functions to deceive. This might be the case when people smile and exclaim over gifts they don't like because they don't want to hurt the feelings of the givers.

4. List ten types of nonverbal communication and an example of how each is commonly used.

Ten different types of nonverbal communication include kinesics, face and eyes, paralanguage, touch, physical attractiveness, clothing, proxemics, chronemics, territory, and environment. Kinesics, posture, and movement convey attitudes (confident or hesitant) and intentions (gestures to indicate what we want). Face and eyes communicate involvement and interest—or lack thereof—when making or refusing to make eye contact. Paralanguage emphasizes words or phrases and also reveals emotion. Touch increases self-disclosure, compliance, and liking, and it improves children's development. Physical attractiveness increases favorable ratings in personal and professional encounters. Clothing communicates status in various situations, from wearing uniforms to having the latest brand name on your jeans. Proxemics can communicate your view of a relationship and establish closeness. In U.S. culture, behaviors that indicate you expect to be waited on quickly send chronemic messages of high status. Territorial behaviors send messages with regard to respect and status: a higher-status person invades another's territory more readily than a lower-status person. Different environments communicate the types of behavior expected. For instance, a classroom arranged in a circle or horseshoe "tells" students to interact, whereas desks facing the front "say" pay attention, face the front, and avoid interacting with others.

5. Describe important categories communicators use in describing distance and voice (proxemics and paralanguage).

Edward T. Hall's categorizations of distances at which people communicate include the intimate distance of zero to eighteen inches, the distance at which you can be slapped or kissed. The personal distance of eighteen inches to four feet is the distance at which personal conversations are usually conducted. The social distance of four to twelve feet is used for business conversations, and at the public distance of beyond twelve feet less-personal interactions, such as lectures, occur.

Categories used to describe the features of paralanguage include the tone, speed, pitch, volume, and use of pauses and disfluencies. A rising tone and/or disfluencies indicate lack of certainty, a question, or lack of authority. A falling tone indicates a command, authority, or certainty. Loudness may indicate control, certainty, or a desire for attention.

Chapter 5 Answers to Thinking Outside the Box

1. Both language (Chapter 3) and nonverbal communication are described as ambiguous. Compare and contrast the reasons for each being labeled ambiguous.

*Language is ambiguous because the meanings reside in people, not in the words and because there are so many types of troublesome language. The higher on the **abstraction ladder** a word is, the more ambiguous it is. Other words are ambiguous by their very nature: **equivocal words**, **relative words,** and **equivocations**. Like language, nonverbal communication is ambiguous because of individual interpretations. The "definition" is in the receiver. A look means one thing to one person and that may be very different from the sender's intent. Both troublesome language and nonverbal communication are ambiguous because it is the decoding that varies from person to person. Although meanings of words are in people, there are some common definitions expressed in a dictionary. Nonverbal behaviors don't even come with a "dictionary" of common meanings. [Boldfaced words are from Chapter 3.]*

2. How can perception checks (Chapter 2) help you to be a more effective nonverbal communicator?

*Chapter 2 presents the **perception check** as a way of clarifying or checking our understanding of someone's behavior. Thus, it is a useful tool for understanding others' nonverbal messages. Attempting to describe someone's behavior without judging it necessitates awareness of and attention to another's actions. If his or her behavior is unconscious, the description of the behavior brings it to the awareness of both persons, as in this description: "When you snap your gum while we're studying." Stating two possible interpretations reminds you that there may be several* *equally valid interpretations, so rather than prejudge, you learn to withhold judgment. Both the person doing the perception check and the person whose behavior is questioned become aware of the behavior. Since much nonverbal communication is unintentional and we are unaware of it, perception checks open the door to discussion. By asking others to clarify their nonverbal communication, you become a better and more accurate interpreter of others' nonverbal behaviors. When others use perception checks to clarify our behavior, we can become more effective nonverbal communicators by eliminating those behaviors we don't want to engage in and clarifying our intentions with regard to other behaviors. [Boldfaced words are from Chapter 2.]*

CHAPTER 6   UNDERSTANDING INTERPERSONAL RELATIONSHIPS

SQ3R in Action

Generate an SQ3R chart for this chapter here: www.teach-nology.com/web_tools/ graphic_org/sq3r/

Survey

Skim the title, Chapter Highlights, objectives ("You should understand" and "You should be able to"), headings, tables, photos, cartoons, figures, charts, and items in the margin. Glance at the titles of the Critical Thinking Probes and Ethical Challenges. At the end of each chapter, look over the list of Key Terms, Activities, and Resources.

Question

Ask yourself questions. What do you know about these topics from your own life experiences and from other classes? Ask these six questions in each section: who, what, when, where, how, and why.

Read

Take one heading at a time and read to find the answers to the questions you've posed.

Recite

In your own words, say the answer aloud and then write it out.

Review

Review each section and then review the whole chapter. This is a good time to use the activities at the end of each chapter and the activities and the sample exams on the CD-ROM. Remember to periodically review the previous chapters as well.

Chapter 6 Outline

(Italicized words are key terms.)
I.   A first step toward understanding interpersonal relationships is identifying their essential characteristics.
   A. Two people (a dyad) comprise a *contextual interpersonal relationship*; however, a *qualitative interpersonal relationship* has qualities of uniqueness and distinctiveness that are not true of just any two people.
   B. Interpersonal communication on the Internet can be both quantitatively and qualitatively interpersonal, in spite of limited face-to-face time.

C. Interpersonal messages have both *content* and *relational messages* (verbal and nonverbal cues about the level of *affinity*, *respect*, *immediacy*, and *control* in the relationship).

D. *Metacommunication* (communicating about communication) can play a role in resolving conflicts and reinforcing relationships.

II. *Intimacy* is a unique facet of interpersonal relationships.

A. Intimacy may be physical, intellectual, or emotional or may involve shared activities.

B. Gender seems to create different perceptions of what intimacy is and different values with regard to expressing intimacy, either verbally or through shared activity.

C. Cultural differences, particularly between collectivist and individualist cultures, result in varying expectations and expressions of intimacy.

III. Relationships aren't easy to portray in one simple model, so scholars use several models of relational development and maintenance.

A. *Developmental models* demonstrate stages of relationships that develop over time from initiating to bonding to terminating.

B. *Dialectical models* of relational maintenance illustrate *dialectical tensions* and strategies for coping with them.

C. Models account for change and movement that are characteristic of relationships.

IV. *Self-disclosure* in interpersonal relationships involves sharing information that is deliberate, significant, and not known by others.

A. The *social penetration model* illustrates the relationship of the *breadth* and *depth* of self-disclosure in a relationship.

B. The *Johari Window* model illustrates the amount and correlation of open, blind, hidden, and unknown aspects of relationships.

C. The dynamics of self-disclosure include cultural influences as well as its dyadic, symmetrical, and incremental nature.

D. Guidelines for appropriate self-disclosure include considerations about the relationship, the other person, and the risks, relevance, appropriateness, reciprocity, constructiveness, and clarity of the disclosure,

E. Widely used alternatives to self-disclosure include lies (including *altruistic lies*), *equivocal language,* and hints.

Chapter 6 Summary

Exploring and studying interpersonal relationships is a complex endeavor because there are so many variables in interpersonal relationships. Any relationship consisting of two people can be called contextually interpersonal, but a relationship is qualitatively interpersonal only when each person sees the other as unique and irreplaceable. The person who waits on you in the bookstore could readily be replaced by any other; the sister with whom you share your life's experiences could not be replaced by another because of the distinctiveness of your relationship.

All messages have both content and relational dimensions, and it is the relational messages that signifying the degree of control, respect, immediacy, and affinity between the communicators. Metacommunication, or communication about communication, contributes to participants' discussion of their relational experiences.

Intimacy is a word used to describe special elements of relationships, although the word may have different meanings and value for men than for women. The meaning also varies across cultures, since some cultures define intimacy quite differently and value some types of intimacy more than others. Differences in collectivist and individualist cultures' behaviors regarding levels and targets of self-disclosure are especially noteworthy.

Interpersonal relationships are described and characterized through the lenses of various relational models. Developmental models, like that proposed by Mark Knapp, look at stages of relationships as they develop over time. He proposes that common but not always universal stages of relationships are initiating, experimenting, intensifying, integrating, bonding, differentiating, circumscribing, stagnating, avoiding, and terminating. Rather than look at stages of relationships, dialectical models describe the strains involved in relationships by identifying common dialectical tensions—those seemingly contradictory yet mutually desirable outcomes. Often relational partners want openness and privacy, predictability and novelty, and connection and autonomy. How do relational partners handle these tensions? Usually in one of these eight ways: denial, disorientation, selection, alternation, segmentation, moderation, reframing, or reaffirmation.

All models have this in common: No one model totally explains all of the elements of interpersonal relationships. Change and variation among relationships and within a particular relationship are normal. Change or movement always takes participants to a new place in their relationship.

Self-disclosure has been studied extensively in interpersonal relationships. It means voluntarily and purposefully sharing significant and otherwise unknown information about yourself with another person.

One model that explains how self-disclosure operates is the social penetration model, which classifies disclosures according to their breadth (the variety of topics disclosed) and depth (viewed from superficial to deeper levels: cliché, fact, opinion, and feeling). Another model, the Johari Window, looks at the relationship as a window with four panes, representing open, hidden, blind, or unknown aspects of the relationship. In this model, increased disclosure creates a larger open pane and a smaller hidden pane. Receiving feedback (listening to others) increases the size of the open pane and reduces the size of the blind pane. This window will have different-sized panes, depending on the level of disclosure.

Understanding characteristics of self-disclosure helps relational partners create optimum levels of disclosure in relationships. Because people from different cultures may value or desire self-disclosure in dissimilar ways, intercultural relational partners may disagree about the appropriateness of and ideal level of disclosure. Disclosure usually occurs in dyads, symmetrically and incrementally, so it follows that if you desire more disclosure but never spend time alone with a person and never disclose to him or her, chances of disclosure decrease. A parent who wants more self-disclosure from a child increases the chances of that happening by ensuring time alone with the child and sharing him or herself with the child. On the other hand, if you want to minimize self-disclosure from a colleague or neighbor, minimize time alone with that person and do not automatically reciprocate their disclosures.

It is difficult to determine the right amount of self-disclosure in any relationship; however, reflecting on these questions helps guide you: Is the other person important to you? Is the risk reasonable? Are the amounts and types of disclosure appropriate? Is the disclosure relevant, reciprocated, clear, and understandable? Will the effect be constructive?

Self-disclosure is always a choice for communicators. Researchers find that people often do consider and choose other options, such as lies, equivocations, and hints.

This chapter explored several ways to understand interpersonal relationships. These included looking at key characteristics of relationships, the role of intimacy in relationships, and several models that help make sense of relational development and depth. In addition, the chapter developed insights into the role of self-disclosure in relationships and guidelines for creating optimum levels of self-disclosure in your relationships.

Chapter 6 Key Terms

For each of these terms, define the term, give an example, and explain the significance of the term.

1. affinity

2. altruistic lies

3. breadth (of self-disclosure)

4. content messages

5. contextually interpersonal communication

6. control

7. depth (of self-disclosure)

8. developmental model

9. dialectical model (of relational maintenance)

10. dialectical tensions

11. equivocal language

12. immediacy

13. intimacy

14. Johari Window

15. metacommunication

16. qualitative interpersonal communication

17. relational messages

18. respect

19. self-disclosure

20. social penetration model

Chapter 6 Review Questions

These questions are designed to help you understand this chapter's concepts and express your understanding in your own words. For practice with true/false and multiple-choice questions, use the CD-ROM you received with the text.

1. What is the relationship between metacommunication and relational messages?

2. Describe the major influences on a person's understanding of intimacy.

3. Compare and contrast the Knapp and the Johari Window models.

4. What is the correlation between the most common reasons for self-disclosing and the guidelines for effective and appropriate self-disclosure?

5. Give examples of your own or others' use of lies, equivocations, and hints with reference to the function each served.

Chapter 6 Thinking Outside the Box: Synthesizing Your Knowledge

These questions are designed to help you develop the big picture by blending what you've learned in this chapter and elsewhere.

1. Review Chapter 3's discussion of language. What correlation do you see in that chapter's consideration of problem language and this chapter's discussion of alternatives to self-disclosure?

2. How does this chapter's discussion of dialectical tensions relate to Chapter 1's discussion of communication competence?

Chapter 6 Answers to Review Questions

1. What is the correlation between metacommunication and relational messages?

Metacommunication refers to interaction about one's patterns and styles of communication. Relational messages are cues embedded in every message that reveal communicators' views and feelings about each other. Relational messages convey beliefs about communicators' perceived levels of control, respect, affinity, and immediacy for each other. Both metacommunication and relational messages communicate about the relationship. Additionally, metacommunication carries relational messages. "We need to talk about this relationship right now" is a message high in control and low in respect compared to "When would be a good time to talk?" The former lacks respect for the other person's time and demands, rather than requests, a discussion. Since relational messages are contained in all messages, by definition, metacommunication contains relational messages, and they are often more overt than in other types of communication.

2. Describe the major influences on one's understanding of intimacy.

Definitions of intimacy vary, and while some people conclude that physical intimacy is of primary importance, others opt for intellectual intimacy, emotional intimacy, or shared activities. All can promote sharing and bonding. Gender also influences views of intimacy. Women value self-disclosure more than men, so it follows that women might place greater value on intimacy resulting from verbal disclosure, while men tend to create intimacy through shared activities. Cultural norms prescribe the value of intimacy, the types of relationships in which it is desirable, and the acceptable means of expressing intimacy. Cultural norms vary with regard to the desirability of expressing intimacy verbally, physically, publicly, or privately.

3. Compare and contrast the Knapp and the Johari Window models.

The Knapp model is a developmental model of relationships depicting the stages that are characteristic of many relationships. The Johari Window is a model to look at the degree of self-disclosure in a relationship. Both models examine the status of relationships; the Knapp model categorizes stages of relationships, while the Johari Window explores the amount of openness in relationships. The Knapp model can reveal whether a relationship is in a coming-apart stage and can lead to strategies to repair the relationship and reenter a more bonded stage. The Johari Window model depicts the size of open, hidden, blind, or unknown areas of relationships that people might desire to enlarge or reduce. If there is movement in one model, there would likely be change or movement in the other model. So, these two models emphasize change in different elements of relationships.

4. What is the correlation between the most common reasons for self-disclosing and the guidelines for effective and appropriate self-disclosure?

    Answers will vary and will draw on these basics. Reasons frequently cited to explain why people self-disclose include catharsis, self-clarification, self-validation, reciprocity, impression management, relational maintenance and enhancement, and control. Guidelines for self-disclosure include (a) Is the other person important to you? (b) Is the risk of disclosing reasonable? (c) Are the amount and type of disclosure appropriate? (d) Is the disclosure relevant? (e) Is the disclosure reciprocated? (f) Will the effect be constructive? and (g) Is the disclosure clear and understandable?

    First, a correlation exists with regard to reciprocity: Reciprocity is given as a reason why many people disclose and is also one of the guidelines (e) to consider. Second, relational maintenance is a reason for disclosure, and guideline (f) asks if the effect of the disclosure will be constructive. This implies that people want disclosure to have a positive effect on maintaining and improving relationships and that they disclose because they believe there will be a positive effect. The third correlation seems like a contradiction. Three rather self-centered reasons people self-disclose include catharsis, self-clarification, and validation. If people are disclosing for those reasons, it seems that they are ignoring guidelines (a) and (b) and are not considering the importance of the other person or the risks of disclosure.

5. Give examples of your own or others' use of lies, equivocations, and hints with reference to the function each served.

    Answers will vary greatly and will revolve around these basics: Lies are a distortion of the truth, equivocations try not to reveal a true attitude by using language that has at least two very different meanings, and hints are a very indirect way to state something. Samples: I lied when I didn't completely understand the technician explaining my computer repair to me. I didn't want to take any more time to have it explained to me. So I said I understood, because I understood enough for my purposes, but not to the extent the technician desired. The year my brother was in a drug treatment program, my parents' holiday letter used equivocation in saying that Joe was "taking time off from college, learning about himself and finding his way." That was as much of the truth as they wanted many people to know and it wasn't a lie. It saved face for both Joe and my parents. I hint when I don't want to tell my friends I don't have money for some of the things they can afford. If they suggest high-priced activities (dinner at an expensive restaurant), I'll hint that I want to save money or that I had a different activity (a video and pizza) in mind. I hope they'll change their minds without me revealing my whole financial picture.

Chapter 6 Answers to Thinking Outside the Box

1. Review Chapter 3's discussion of language. What correlation is there in that chapter's consideration of problem language and this chapter's discussion of alternatives to self-disclosure?

   The strongest correlation is in each chapter's development of the concept of **equivocation.** *Chapter 3 considers* **equivocal words** *to be language that is ambiguous and causes confusion. Here that notion is added on to by suggesting that instead of self-disclosure (truthful statements about oneself), equivocation is an alternative used to save face or avoid hurt. So both chapters would agree that equivocation can cause confusion and isn't completely truthful. [Boldfaced words are from Chapter 3.]*

2. How does this chapter's discussion of dialectical tensions relate to Chapter 1's discussion of communication competence?

   Chapter 1 suggests that **communication competence** *is relational and that what people consider satisfying and appropriate varies with each relationship, particularly if the relationship is intercultural. Dialectical tensions are relational strains resulting from the desire to achieve diametrically opposed relational goals. The discussion of communication competence is aimed at helping communicators understand that two people may measure relational satisfaction in different ways and judge relationship success by different markers. The discussion of dialectical tensions illuminates the process of striving for opposing goals (i.e., connection and autonomy) at the same time. Communication competence is enhanced if communicators recognize that each has intrapersonal dialectical tensions and differing interpersonal goals and strategies. [Boldfaced words are from Chapter 1.]*

CHAPTER 7   IMPROVING INTERPERSONAL COMMUNICATION

SQ3R in Action

Generate an SQ3R chart for this chapter here: www.teach-nology.com/web_tools/ graphic_org/sq3r/

Survey

Skim the title, Chapter Highlights, objectives ("You should understand" and "You should be able to"), headings, tables, photos, cartoons, figures, charts, and items in the margin. Glance at the titles of the Critical Thinking Probes and Ethical Challenges. At the end of each chapter, look over the list of Key Terms, Activities, and Resources.

Question

Ask yourself questions. What do you know about these topics from your own life experiences and from other classes? Ask these six questions in each section: who, what, when, where, how, and why.

Read

Take one heading at a time and read to find the answers to the questions you've posed.

Recite

In your own words, say the answer aloud and then write it out.

Review

Review each section and then review the whole chapter. This is a good time to use the activities at the end of each chapter and the activities and the sample exams on the CD-ROM. Remember to periodically review the previous chapters as well.

Chapter 7 Outline

(Italicized words are key terms.)

I. *Communication climates* develop from the types of messages and reflect how valued people feel; in turn, the type of climate adds to or detracts from relational satisfaction.
   A. Climate is shaped by confirming or disconfirming messages.
      1. *Confirming responses* are those of recognition, acknowledgment, and endorsement.
      2. *Disconfirming responses* may be a matter of perception and are frequently messages of disagreeing, ignoring, and distancing.
   B. Relational climates are formed by words or behaviors and are reinforced by

conflict *spirals* (*escalatory* or *deescalatory*).

    C. According to *Gibb's* categories, different types of messages create either supportive or defensive *communication climates.*

        1. Messages perceived as containing evaluation, control, strategy, neutrality, superiority, and certainty contribute to a defensive climate.

        2. Messages that are perceived as descriptive, problem oriented, spontaneous, empathic, equal, and provisional promote a supportive climate.

II. One of the great challenges in relationships is to manage interpersonal *conflict.*

    A. Conflict is defined as an expressed struggle, in which there is interdependence and perceived incompatible goals, perceived scarce rewards, or interference from a third party.

    B. Conflict is expressed in one of five major styles: *nonassertion* (includes avoidance and accommodation), *direct aggression, passive aggression ("crazymaking"), indirect communication,* or *assertion.*

    C. An assertive clear message consists of a description of behavior; an interpretation of that behavior (may include a perception check); a description of feelings; a description of consequences for you, the other person, or third parties; and an intention (where you stand, requests of others, or your future action plan).

    D. Gender differences in conflict styles often begin in childhood and continue as adults

    E. Cultural influences such as individualistic or collectivist culture, high- or low-context, and ethnicity all affect approaches to conflict.

    F. Common methods of conflict resolution are win–lose, lose–lose, compromise, and win–win.

    G. *Win–win problem solving* involves these steps: identify problem and needs, make a date to discuss the problem, describe the problem and needs of both parties, check each other's understanding of needs, negotiate a solution, and follow up on the solution.

Chapter 7 Summary

The climate of a relationship and the parties' approaches to conflict significantly affect the level of satisfaction that people experience in relationships.

The climate of a relationship reflects the degree to which people feel that they matter and are valued in a relationship. Climates are shaped by confirming or disconfirming messages, by conflict spirals, and by supportive or defensive messages. Confirming messages are those that increase our sense of being valued by others and include messages that recognize, acknowledge, and endorse people. They create a sense of validation and importance. In contrast, disconfirming messages deny another person's value or significance and include messages that disagree with, attack, or ignore someone.

Another way to think about building relational climates is to consider whether messages contribute to a defensive or supportive climate. According to the Gibb categories, if a message you send is perceived by someone as evaluative, controlling, or strategic (manipulative), the other will likely become defensive. This is especially true if the other believes you have no right to evaluate or control them. Messages that lack empathy are labeled neutral, and they also contribute to a defensive climate. Here the term neutral means indifferent or uncaring, not fair-minded. Defensiveness arises from messages of superiority and certainty as well. So these six kinds of messages likely create defensiveness. Gibb also considers six other kinds of messages that that will more likely create supportive climates. Messages that are perceived as descriptive, problem oriented, spontaneous, empathic, equal, and provisional contribute to a supportive climate. You can do this in several ways: using "I" language, trying to solve problems rather than blame others, treating all people as equally deserving of respect, and showing concern for others' feelings and beliefs. Taking time to create a supportive climate is more satisfying than ignoring the relational climate and trying to overcome the adverse effects of a defensive climate. It is easier to deal with conflict, our next topic, in the context of a supportive climate.

Conflict is a normal part of relationships. Each partner's conflict style and approach shape a relationship. Conflict occurs when two parties are interdependent and see each other as having goals that are not compatible, or one or both perceive a lack of reward (physical or emotional) or interference from someone or something outside the relationship. Conflict styles often fit one of five patterns: nonassertion, direct aggression, passive aggression (also called crazymaking), indirect communication, or assertion. A person using a nonassertive style does not insist on or stand up for his or her own point of view and often gives in to another party. A person using a directly aggressive style often doesn't respect or consider the other at all and uses power or force to get his or her own way. A person using a passive–aggressive style doesn't appear aggressive on the surface but takes aggressive actions behind the scenes, so issues aren't dealt with up front. A person using an indirect communication style may hint or use a middle person but not deal with the conflict directly. Finally, a person using an assertive style is respectful of the other person while at the same time directly speaking for and getting one's own needs met.

One way to express conflict assertively is to use a clear message in which you describe the behavior of the other without blame or judgment; you express your interpretation of this behavior. At this point, you might also use a perception check in which you check with your partner to understand their interpretation of the event or behavior. A clear message goes on to state your feelings, the consequences you or others experienced as a result of the behavior, and your intention. Intention statements might include what you want from the other person, what you intend to do, or where you stand on the issue.

Gender and culture differences shape people's approach to conflict. The gender differences can be identified in childhood and they appear to continue into adulthood. Males tend to use more-powerful directives, commands, and aggressive behaviors, whereas females seem more comfortable using cooperative behaviors, such as requesting and explaining, in order to maintain relationships. Cultural differences are most obvious in contrasting attitudes toward conflict in individualist, low-context societies versus those in collectivist, high-context societies. People in the first tend to be more assertive and value dealing directly and openly with conflict. Persons from the second prefer face-saving, indirect means of approaching conflict.

Persons engaged in conflict usually employ one of four methods of conflict resolution. A person employing a win–lose manner attempts to resolve conflicts competitively, as contests to be won with power. This approach sees the goal as winning for oneself and making the other person lose. One way the lose–lose approach occurs is when one person perceives herself as the loser in a win–lose conflict and decides to bring the other person down with her. This ensures that no one will win. A compromise occurs when parties seem unable to reach their goals entirely, but each side gives up part of what they wanted in order to get some other part. A compromise is an outcome that does not entirely meet the needs of both parties but may be the best outcome the parties can achieve. Win–win outcomes result when both parties work earnestly to understand and satisfy each other's needs without damaging the self-respect of either.

Achieving a win–win outcome is not a quick and easy process, but it can be achieved by using communication skills to accomplish each step of the process. The first steps are to identify the problem and the unmet needs, make a mutually agreeable date to problem solve, and take time for each party to describe the problem and needs from his or her perspective. After each description, each person checks that he or she heard and understood the other. Finally, a solution can be negotiated by carefully identifying and defining the conflict, generating many possible solutions, evaluating the solutions and deciding on the best one. Last, both parties should make a plan and follow up on the solution.

Chapter 7 Key Terms

For each of these terms, define the term, give an example, and explain the significance of the term.

1. assertion

2. certainty

3. communication climate

4. compromise

5. confirming response

6. conflict

7. controlling message

8. crazymaking

9. deescalatory conflict spiral

10. descriptive communication

11. direct aggression

12. disconfirming response

13. empathy

14. equality

15. escalatory conflict spiral

16. evaluative communication

17. Gibb categories

18. "I" language

19. indirect communication

20. lose–lose problem solving

21. neutrality

22. nonassertion

23. passive aggression

24. problem orientation

25. provisionalism

26. spiral

27. spontaneity

28. strategy

29. superiority

30. win–lose conflicts

31. win–win problem solving

32. "you" language

Chapter 7 Review Questions

These questions are designed to help you understand this chapter's concepts and express your understanding in your own words. For practice with true/false and multiple-choice questions, use the CD-ROM you received with the text.

1. Describe the types of messages that contribute to confirming and disconfirming climates.

2. How do these styles of conflict differ: nonassertive, directly aggressive, passive–aggressive, indirect, and assertive.

3. When dealing with conflict, what cultural and gender issues need to be considered?

4. How do win–lose, lose–lose, compromise, and win–win approaches to conflict differ?

5. Choose a specific conflict situation and explain how an assertive message in the behavior-interpretation-feeling-consequence-intention format can be helpful in that situation.

Chapter 7 Thinking Outside the Box: Synthesizing Your Knowledge

These questions are designed to help you develop the big picture by blending what you've learned in this chapter and elsewhere.

1. Compare and contrast the perception check presented in Chapter 2 with the clear message presented in this chapter.

2. Give specific examples of at least three types of nonverbal behaviors (Chapter 5) that could contribute to supportive or defensive climates as categorized by Gibb.

Chapter 7 Answers to Review Questions

1. Describe the types of messages that contribute to confirming and disconfirming climates.

Messages that pay attention to and recognize others, that acknowledge and endorse them, create confirming climates. Saying hello, affirming others' presence and contributions, and agreeing with others are examples of these types of messages. Messages that contribute to disconfirming climates include those that clearly indicate disagreement, those that ignore or fail to acknowledge another, and those that put distance—emotional or physical—between people.

2. How do these styles of conflict differ: nonassertive, directly aggressive, passive–aggressive, indirect, and assertive?

Each style of conflict takes a different approach to getting one's needs met. A nonassertive approach allows others to have their way and their say without regard for your needs or desires. It doesn't make waves and may even allow oneself to be taken advantage of. A directly aggressive approach meets your needs without regard for others' needs, wants, or feelings. A passive–aggressive approach may appear calm or submissive on the surface, but underneath or behind the scenes some very forceful, inconsiderate behavior occurs. These behaviors can be quite dysfunctional and have earned the label "crazymaking." An indirect approach hints at or tries to get needs met without ever clarifying them. An assertive response differs from the others in that it considers the needs and feelings of both parties. The attitude is that both parties are important and both matter. There is a respect and equality implied in every conflict.

3. When dealing with conflict, what cultural and gender issues need to be considered?

Socialization from childhood often creates patterns for approaching conflicts that men and women carry on into adulthood. Women direct their attention to maintaining relationships with messages of cooperation, while men more often use messages that are more task related and directive. Men might be described as more task oriented while women are more socially oriented. Men and women would do well to understand what is important to each other and work from that understanding. One cultural influence that needs to be considered is whether persons engaged in conflict are from a high- or low-context culture. This might affect whether either party wants to approach the conflict in a direct or indirect way. Another consideration is that persons from a collectivist culture tend to be less direct than those from an individualist culture.

4. How do win–lose, lose–lose, compromise, and win–win approaches to conflict differ?

A win–lose approach is competitive and the person with this approach sees a conflict as a power struggle to be won. A lose–lose approach occurs when one person believes he or she is losing (often because of someone's win–lose approach) and acts in such a way that ensures the other person loses, too. Or, often when people already believe they cannot win, they approach conflict with the goal of being sure the others lose rather than see others win. Compromise occurs when two parties believe there is no way for them both to achieve their goals, so each gives in some and gives up something. Neither party's needs nor wants are fully met; each loses something. A win–win approach rests on an underlying belief that both parties' needs can be met. The approach looks for creative ways that each party can meet his or her needs while maintaining dignity and respect for the other.

5. Choose a specific conflict situation and explain how an assertive message in the behavior-interpretation-feeling-consequence-intention format can be helpful in that situation.

Answers will vary and should include a conflict situation in which the source of conflict is clear (some goals that were incompatible with someone else's, some interference with your goals from someone else, or not enough of something to go around). Then the assertive message should state the behavior of the other in a descriptive, nonjudgmental way; give an interpretation of what you think the behavior means; state your feeling without blaming someone else for it; show what the result of the behavior was for you, the other person, or third persons; and then state an intention that clarifies what you intend to do, what you want others to do, or what your strong belief is. In a conflict over the use of a shared car, a statement might sound like this, "When you keep the car past the time you said you would, I think you're inconsiderate and I feel annoyed. I end up stressed and late for class. I want you to return the car at the agreed-on time." Using this message might prevent defensiveness on the part of the other person and allow him or her to respond and correct the behavior. It allows both persons to pursue a win–win solution.

Chapter 7 Answers to Thinking Outside the Box

1. Compare and contrast the perception check presented in Chapter 2 with the clear message presented in this chapter.

*Both clear messages and **perception checks** are example of skills valuable in **low-context cultures** (Chapter 3) because both employ language to try to clarify behaviors and interpretations. The difference is that the perception check is used when you want to understand someone else's words or actions and the clear message is used when you want someone else to understand your interpretation, feelings, consequences, and intentions. [Boldfaced words are from Chapters 2 and 3.]*

2. Give specific examples of at least three types of nonverbal behaviors (Chapter 5) that could contribute to supportive or defensive climates as categorized by Gibb.

*Not responding to a friend's or co-worker's phone call for a long time (or not ever) would send a **chronemic** message that would contribute to a climate of defensiveness. It is likely that the other person would perceive that you didn't care for him (neutrality) or that he was not worthy for you to respond to (superiority). Using touch to hug a friend could send a message of spontaneity and empathy and contributes to a supportive climate. If used to generate sarcasm or condescension, **paralanguage** might send a message perceived as superior, controlling, or neutral and create greater defensiveness. [Boldfaced words are from Chapter 5.]*

CHAPTER 8 THE NATURE OF GROUPS

SQ3R in Action

Generate an SQ3R chart for this chapter here: www.teach-nology.com/web_tools/graphic_org/sq3r/

Survey

Skim the title, Chapter Highlights, objectives ("You should understand" and "You should be able to"), headings, tables, photos, cartoons, figures, charts, and items in the margin. Glance at the titles of the Critical Thinking Probes and Ethical Challenges. At the end of each chapter, look over the list of Key Terms, Activities, and Resources.

Question

Ask yourself questions. What do you know about these topics from your own life experiences and from other classes? Ask these six questions in each section: who, what, when, where, how, and why.

Read

Take one heading at a time and read to find the answers to the questions you've posed.

Recite

In your own words, say the answer aloud and then write it out.

Review

Review each section and then review the whole chapter. This is a good time to use the activities at the end of each chapter and the activities and the sample exams on the CD-ROM. Remember to periodically review the previous chapters as well.

Chapter 8 Outline

(Italicized words are key terms.)

I. A small *group* consists of five to seven members who are interdependent, have common goals, and interact over time.

II. *Individual goals* might vary from or be consistent with *group goals.*

    A. Individual goals may have a *task orientation* or a *social orientation.*

    B. Individual goals not shared by or with the group are termed a *hidden agenda.*

III. There are a variety of types of groups, each with different purposes, including *learning groups, growth groups, problem-solving groups,* and *social groups.*

IV. Groups exhibit certain characteristics such as *rules, norms, roles*, and decision-making patterns.
- A. Rules and norms differ.
    1. Rules are usually formal and often written.
    2. Norms are interaction patterns *(social, procedural,* and *task norms)* and can be identified by habitual behaviors of group members and punishment of violations.
- B. Roles emerge from repetitive behaviors of group members; these may be *formal roles* or *informal roles* that include *task roles, social/maintenance roles*, and *dysfunctional roles*.
- C. Groups' patterns of interaction are described mathematically by *sociograms* and by *networks*, such as *all-channel, chain*, and *wheel* (utilizing a *gatekeeper*) networks.
- D. Groups make decisions in many ways that include *consensus*, majority control, expert opinion, minority control, and authority rule; the most effective method depends on the type and importance of the decision and the time available for decision making.

V. Five major cultural variations influence group communication.
- A. Persons from cultures with an *individualistic orientation* are less likely to feel loyalty to a group or gain identity from a group than persons from cultures with a *collectivistic orientation*.
- B. Persons from low *power distance* cultures expect less hierarchy within groups than persons from cultures where high power distance is the norm.
- C. Groups members from cultures with high *uncertainty avoidance* are less likely to take risks, more likely to avoid conflict, and less likely to accept change than group members from cultures with low uncertainty avoidance.
- D. A group functions with different norms regarding work and socialization depending on whether members have a greater task or social orientation.
- E. Whether group members have a short- or long-term orientation affects their approach and timing toward their expectation about reaching goals.

Chapter 8 Summary

Most of us belong to and interact with many groups in our personal and professional lives. Your satisfaction and effectiveness in groups can be improved if you understand how groups operate.

On the surface, it may not be easy to distinguish a group from just any gathering of people; however, a group's size, interdependence, and interaction over time make it distinct. Unlike people who just work or play beside each other, groups consist of three to twenty people who interact in purposeful ways over time and whose behaviors, for better or worse, affect each other.

Group effectiveness or ineffectiveness is affected by the interplay of members' individual goals and the group goals. Individual goals may be task oriented (focused on a specific job) or socially oriented (focused on belonging, being liked, or exerting influence). When group goals and individual goals are in sync, both the group and the individual are likely to be satisfied. However, when an individual's goals are incompatible with stated group goals, serious problems may result. Hidden agendas, those individual goals not stated upfront, can create difficulties for the group and interfere with the attainment of group goals.

People choose to belong to different kinds of groups for various reasons. Learning groups increase members' skills or knowledge in a particular area, such as sports, politics, or literature. Growth groups assist members in dealing with personal issues by offering support and information from others in the group. Problem-solving groups operate on many levels, from planning the family reunion to passing hand-gun legislation. Social groups are formal or informal groups whose key objective is to meet the social needs of members, such as a need to belong, be cared for, or have some sway.

To be an effective group member, strive to understand group dynamics. Begin with identifying group rules, norms, and roles. Rules are the officially stated or written codes that groups operate under. Norms are those unstated but clearly understood policies that group members abide by. A rule might state that the group meets Monday evenings; the norm might be that profanity is never used by members at meetings. Norms might be social (using first names), procedural (processes used for decisions), or task oriented (note taking, mission-related issues). Roles are patterns of anticipated behavior from group members and may be formal or informal. Formal roles are clearly designated and named, such as president or committee chair. Informal roles are either task or social roles that keep the group functioning. Task roles, including information giver, initiator, and coordinator, move groups to succeed in their jobs. Social roles, such as harmonizer or supporter, help group members feel included and cared for. Dysfunctional roles interfere with a group's work, and their presence can spell disaster for group effectiveness. You can improve your effectiveness in a group by looking for essential, unfilled roles and filling them. Avoid roles that aren't needed or are already adequately filled, and avoid dysfunctional roles at all costs.

Group interactions are numerically and interactively complex. A sociogram is a diagram that illustrates the participation of members by showing who interacted with whom. Network diagrams show some common interaction patterns among group members. The all-channel network shows equal participation of members, while in a wheel network a gatekeeper serves as a dispatcher, conveying messages among members. The chain network reveals each person as a link in a chain, with information passed from one person to another. Understanding these patterns helps you determine whether the patterns that exist are contributing to effective or ineffective functioning in a group.

All groups make decisions of one sort or another, and the method used is another distinguishing characteristic of groups. There isn't one best decision-making method; the type, importance, and timing of a decision determine the best method. Common decision-making methods include majority control, consensus, expert opinion, minority control, and authority rule. Majority control is sometimes the only decision-making process that groups in the United States are familiar with, even though it does not produce the best decisions. Consensus takes time for each person to express opinions and feelings until everyone is satisfied with the decision. Experts can be used to make decisions (expert opinion), as can committees or appointees (minority control). Authority rule involves one person deciding for a group.

Groups are increasingly multicultural ventures, and effective participation requires awareness of cultural influences that impact group communication. Group members with collectivistic orientations express loyalty to and gain identity from their primary group affiliations (not from all groups) more so than persons from cultures with an individualistic orientation. Persons from low-power distance cultures like the United States are not comfortable with extreme hierarchies in groups and prefer greater equality among group members than persons from cultures comfortable with high-power distances. Group members from cultures rated high in uncertainty avoidance are more likely to avoid risks, conflict, and change compared to people from cultures with low uncertainty avoidance. Group members may show a greater inclination toward getting the job done (task orientation) or getting along with members (social orientation). Finally, group members may lean toward either a short- or long-term orientation when making decisions, and this could lead to great variations in members' approaches to a problem.

Groups are complex entities, and members will benefit from information and insight with regard to their characteristics, goals, rules, norms, roles, networks, decision-making practices, and cultural influences. Understanding how each of these characteristics of groups operates improves your effectiveness in groups.

Chapter 8 Key Terms

For each of these terms, define the term, give an example, and explain the significance of the term.

1. all-channel network

2. chain network

3. collectivistic orientation

4. consensus

5. dysfunctional roles

6. formal roles

7. gatekeeper

8. group

9. group goals

10. growth groups

11. hidden agenda

12. individual goals

13. individualistic orientation

14. informal roles (functional roles)

15. learning group

16. norms

17. power distance

18. problem-solving groups

19. procedural norms

20. roles

21. rules

22. social groups

23. social norms

24. social orientation

25. social roles

26. sociogram

27. task norms

28. task orientation

29. task roles

30. uncertainty avoidance

31. wheel network

Chapter 8 Review Questions

These questions are designed to help you understand this chapter's concepts and express your understanding in your own words. For practice with true/false and multiple-choice questions, use the CD-ROM you received with the text.

1. How does a group, as defined in this chapter, differ from just a gathering of people?

2. Describe your personal and group goals for groups you are familiar with.

3. Define norms, roles, and interaction patterns. Then describe one of each for groups in which you are or have been a member.

4. Distinguish among the five decision-making methods described in this chapter.

5. Identify several cultural influences that affect communication in groups.

Chapter 8 Thinking Outside the Box: Synthesizing Your Knowledge

These questions are designed to help you develop the big picture by blending what you've learned in this chapter and elsewhere.

1. How does group membership and group communication affect identity management (Chapter 2)?

2. Discuss three ways in which paying attention to principles of language use (Chapter 3) can be used to improve group communication.

Chapter 8 Answers to Review Questions

1. How does a group, as defined in this chapter, differ from just a gathering of people?

People gathered together for an event or working independently side by side do not necessarily possess the characteristics of a group. A group, as defined in this chapter, consists of between three and twenty people who work together interdependently over time. A group of people in the same place at the same time may have no connection or relationship to each other; a group has a common goal or purpose, and each person's work and behavior affects the others. In addition, members interact, not just exist, with each other.

2. Describe your personal and group goals for groups you are familiar with.

Answers will vary. They should distinguish between the individual's goals and group goals and state whether these were shared with the group or constituted a hidden agenda. Group goals should be goals shared by all group members.

Example: I joined the city soccer team Kal's Gals to meet new people and keep in shape. I like to win, but I didn't care about winning every game. Most of my teammates were engaged in a serious rivalry with one of the other city teams, Emil's Angels. They really pushed themselves for those games. I didn't hide the fact that I was new to the city and wanted to meet people (personal goal). My goals didn't stop me from doing well, but I didn't go beyond a certain effort. I contributed to the team but didn't fully share the goal of beating Emil's Angels. Since I didn't share with the group that I wasn't interested in the intense rivalry, this fact might have been a hidden agenda. The group goal was clearly to beat Emil's Angels at all costs.

3. Define norms, roles, and interaction patterns. Then describe one of each for groups in which you are or have been a member.

> *The definition of "norm" should include that norms are the unspoken but strongly abided by rules operating in groups. Example: I was in a group in which one norm was that we all helped clean up after meetings. There was never a committee, no one left until it was done, and no one ever did it alone. We all stayed and helped and we all left together.*
>
> *The definition of "role" is a behavior pattern of an individual within the group. It could fall into the category of a task role, social role, or dysfunctional role. Example: I often take the task role of initiator who says, "Well, let's get started," if we're just chatting. As a social role, I'm often the harmonizer, explaining members' behaviors to each other to soothe hurt feelings.*
>
> *The definition of "interaction patterns" refers to how group members communicate with each other. Example: My study group has a phone tree set up to let each other know when we'll meet or to deal with a problem that comes up. That pattern is a chain network.*

4. Distinguish among the five decision-making methods described in this chapter.

> *Voting and going by the majority is a common pattern, although not always the best pattern for a given situation, especially if the vote is nearly 50–50 and you need commitment and involvement from members. Consensus involves everyone in the discussion and the discussion goes on until all can commit to the decision and feel like they've had their say and have been heard, even if their initial ideas weren't adopted. Authoritative decision making occurs when one person has the power and uses it to make a decision for the whole group. Two other types of decision making are expert opinion, when a group allows someone with experience or information to make the choice, and minority control, in which a group allows a small number (ad hoc appointments or committees, for example) to make the decision for the group.*

5. Identify several cultural influences that affect communication in groups.

> *Cultural patterns that affect communication in groups include the following: Collectivistic or individualistic orientation refers to whether group or individual goals are priorities. High- or low-power distances describe whether people expect and are comfortable with different levels of power and greater hierarchies or greater equality among group members. High or low levels of uncertainty avoidance affect group members' comfort with risks, conflict, and change. Task or social orientation describes whether group members put a priority on getting the work done or maintaining relationships among members. Last, a short- or long-term orientation refers to whether a group member tends to approach problems with solutions that work at the moment only or tends to look for long-term answers. Members whose*

approaches differ on any of these important cultural variables may find themselves in conflict with each other.

Chapter 8 Answers to Thinking Outside the Box

1. How does group membership and group communication affect identity management (Chapter 2)?

   *For many people belonging to a group is a special part of their **impression management**. Groups involve others so they are a public statement of one's **face** or **presenting self**. Your favorite politician probably has strong ties to a particular political party. Think of bands, universities, and religious or military organizations with which people stress their association in order to present a particular identity. People's **self-esteem** rises or falls with acceptance or rejection by a group. So many people make an effort to join groups in order to create an identity, but at other times identities are shaped by the family group one belongs to by birth or adoption. **Significant others** in that family group may influence your **self-concept** as much as the groups you make an effort to join. Group roles are also related to identity management. Whether formal or informal, functional or dysfunctional, group members create identities as critics or initiators or pride themselves on being harmonizers, jokers, or cynics. [Boldfaced words are from Chapter 2.]*

2. Discuss three ways in which paying attention to principles of language use (Chapter 3) can be used to improve group communication.

   Table 3-1 gives examples of powerless language that might prevent your voice from being heard or paid attention to in a group. For instance, using hedges, hesitations, tag questions, and disclaimers could prevent your opinion from being taken seriously or prevent you from being considered for leadership.

   Using "I" language and declarative statements can contribute to group functioning as these types of language indicate that you accept responsibility for your own thoughts and opinions. "You" language might create defensiveness in others, as it sounds like you are blaming. Consider each context carefully and choose the best language to achieve your purpose.

   *Avoid **equivocal words, relative words, slang,** and **jargon** when they cause confusion or prevent important information from being known in group interactions and discussion. Use the appropriate level of **abstraction** to help others understand you. Distinguish **facts** from **opinions** and **inferences** to avoid confusion. **Emotive language** may cause hard feelings and disruptions in task and social functioning in groups. Awareness of gender and culture differences in expectations and use of language can help you participate in group discussions more effectively. [Boldfaced words are from Chapter 3.]*

CHAPTER 9   SOLVING PROBLEMS IN GROUPS

SQ3R in Action

Generate an SQ3R chart for this chapter here: www.teach-nology.com/web_tools/ graphic_org/sq3r/

Survey

Skim the title, Chapter Highlights, objectives ("You should understand" and "You should be able to"), headings, tables, photos, cartoons, figures, charts, and items in the margin. Glance at the titles of the Critical Thinking Probes and Ethical Challenges. At the end of each chapter, look over the list of Key Terms, Activities, and Resources.

Question

Ask yourself questions. What do you know about these topics from your own life experiences and from other classes? Ask these six questions in each section: who, what, when, where, how, and why.

Read

Take one heading at a time and read to find the answers to the questions you've posed.

Recite

In your own words, say the answer aloud and then write it out.

Review

Review each section and then review the whole chapter. This is a good time to use the activities at the end of each chapter and the activities and the sample exams on the CD-ROM. Remember to periodically review the previous chapters as well.

Chapter 9 Outline

(Italicized words are key terms.)

I.   Under certain conditions, groups solve problems better than individuals.
    A.   Advantages of group problem solving include more available resources, potential for greater accuracy, and, with participative decision-making, members' greater commitment to the decision.
    B.   Groups are advantageous in these conditions: the job requires it, there is interdependence among group members, there are multiple solutions possible, and the potential for disagreement is great.
II.   Group problem-solving formats include face-to-face and computer-mediated groups.

A. Face-to-face problem-solving formats include *buzz groups*, *problem census*, *focus groups*, *parliamentary procedure*, *panel discussions*, *symposia*, and *forums*.

B. Computer-mediated groups present advantages and disadvantages.

   1. Advantages include reduced schedule and travel difficulties, possibility of asynchronous communication, and more-balanced participation.

   2. Potential disadvantages include the lack of nonverbal cues, greater time to reach a decision, less-detailed messages due to typing time, and disjointed nature of messages.

III. Groups succeed by following a structured problem-solving method and acknowledging the usual stages of problem-solving groups.

   A. The structured problem-solving approach includes six key steps for members.

      1. Identify the problem or challenge.

      2. Analyze the problem by creating a *probative question*, gathering information, and using a *force field analysis*.

      3. Begin to develop solutions with *brainstorming* or a *nominal group technique*.

      4. Evaluate solutions' desirability, implementation potential, and disadvantages.

      5. Implement a solution by dividing tasks, resources, and responsibilities.

      6. Create a plan to follow up with periodic evaluation and an opportunity to revise as necessary.

   B. Groups typically go through four developmental stages: *orientation, conflict, emergence,* and *reinforcement.*

IV. Groups function effectively when members maintain positive relationships by practicing communication skills and building an optimal level of *cohesiveness.*

   A. Respect, listening, and win–win problem solving skills contribute to positive relationships in groups.

   B. Cohesiveness is built through interdependence; facing outside threats; perception of mutual attractiveness and friendship; shared goals, norms, values, and group experiences; progress toward goals; and lack of perceived internal threats.

V. *Leaders* and *power* in groups are created in several ways.

   A. There are several types of power, and each member of a group may hold one or more types: *legitimate* (or position), *coercive, reward, expert, information,* and *referent power.*

   B. Power is not an either–or characteristic; it is also group-centered and may be distributed among members.

   C. Although some people view leadership through the lens of *trait theories* (you have or don't have the leadership traits) or the *Leadership Grid* (orientation toward task or relationship), the *situational leadership* approach stresses the need to consider the group circumstances and its readiness for a particular *leadership style (authoritarian, democratic, laissez-faire).*

VI. A group's problems with *information underload, information overload,* unequal participation, and conformity need to be addressed.

   A. Unequal participation can be balanced by effective reinforcement, distribution of tasks, and use of nominal group technique to encourage low participants; overparticipation can be discouraged by minimizing unhelpful talk, not reinforcing excessive participation, expressing a desire to hear from others, and challenging irrelevant talk.

   B. *Groupthink* (desire for unanimity overriding critical thinking) can be reduced by reducing status differences of group members and encouraging legitimate disagreement.

Chapter 9 Summary

Small groups are effective for solving problems and performing tasks because of their available resources (both quantitative and qualitative), the potential accuracy of their solutions, and the members' commitments to solutions that result from participative decision making. However, groups aren't *always* ideal for solving problems. They are best used when the problem is beyond the capacity of one person, when tasks are interdependent, when there is more than one possible solution or decision, and when the agreement of members is essential.

Groups use a wide variety of discussion formats when solving problems. Buzz groups, problem censuses, and focus groups are useful at times. Some groups use parliamentary procedure when engaged in decision making. Others use moderated panel discussions, symposia, or forums. Computer-mediated groups simplify time and location issues, minimize status, balance participation, create a permanent record of proceedings, and allow asynchronous communication. They might lose some communication advantages of face-to-face communication such as synchronous nonverbal cues and loss of messages because of the time it takes to type them. Other disadvantages are that messages may seem more disorganized and decisions may take longer. The best format for groups to use will always depend on the characteristics of both the problem and the group. Computer groups can be used to supplement face-to-face groups; they aren't an either–or option.

Groups develop effective solutions to problems when they begin with identifying the problem. In the beginning, it is important to determine and pay attention to open and hidden needs of group members. The next step is to analyze the problem by using probative questions or force field analysis. Next, effective groups develop a number of possible solutions through brainstorming or nominal group technique. It is important not to evaluate possible solutions until a group taps the creativity and contributions of all members. After developing a variety of solutions, groups can evaluate the desirability and feasibility of possible solutions. Then, during the implementation phase, the group monitors its progress and makes sure there is a follow-up plan to revise the solution if necessary.

Most groups go through several stages as they work to solve a problem. First is the orientation stage, during which the members begin to find out about each other. Next, during the conflict stage, members argue and debate various ideas. In the emergence stage, the group moves toward a particular solution. In the reinforcement stage, members sanction the group's decision.

Groups that work well focus not only on the task dimension of their process but on the interactional or relational dimensions as well. Interpersonal issues can often be enhanced or addressed by using listening and conflict-resolution skills. In addition, group cohesiveness and productivity often increase as members develop and progress toward shared goals and develop shared norms and values with no internal threats to each others' identity. Increased cohesiveness often results from the perception of outside threats, from increased interdependence, and from shared group experiences. Groups function best when they understand the importance of maintaining positive relationships.

Leadership is defined as the ability to influence group members through various types of power that any and all group members may possess: legitimate, coercive, reward, expert, information, and referent power. Groups often have nominal leaders who readily share power with other members. Power is not an either–or concept that you either have or don't have. It is better understood along a continuum and by acknowledging that power is group centered and is granted by and distributed among group members.

Leadership can be examined from a variety of perspectives—trait analysis, leadership style, and situational variables. The trait theory of leadership was an early way to consider leadership and looked at traits associated with leaders. Leadership styles may be classified as authoritarian, democratic, or laissez-faire. The Leadership Grid is a way to examine both the task and relational dimensions of leadership and a leader's place along these continuums. Another approach, situational leadership, includes the theory of contingency leadership. Both situational and contingency leadership look at a group's context and preparedness as variables that determine the most effective leadership style for any given context.

Some problems that lessen the effectiveness of small groups include information underload, information overload, unequal participation of group members, and pressure to conform. The advantages of group participation are better attained when group participation is balanced and encouraged. Using the nominal group technique helps encourage participation. Unhelpful talk is discouraged by withholding reinforcement, asserting a desire to hear from others, and challenging the relevance of talk. A danger in group discussion that comes from the pressure to conform is termed "groupthink," a condition that exists when group members strive for unanimity and discourage critical thinking or criticism. Recognizing and reducing groupthink keeps groups more functional.

Understanding group dynamics is a complex process with many related facets. If, as a group member, you understand and can address issues of problem solving, cohesiveness, leadership, power, and participation, you can be a more effective group member.

Chapter 9 Key Terms

For each of these terms, define the term, give an example, and explain the significance of the term.

1. authoritarian leadership style

2. brainstorming

3. buzz group

4. coercive power

5. cohesiveness

6. conflict stage

7. democratic leadership style

8. emergence stage

9. expert power

10. focus group

11. force field analysis

12. forum

13. groupthink

14. information overload

15. information power

16. information underload

17. laissez-faire leadership style

18. leader

19. Leadership Grid

20. legitimate power

21. nominal group technique

22. nominal leader

23. orientation stage

24. panel discussion

25. parliamentary procedure

26. participative decision making

27. power

28. probative question

29. problem census

30. referent power

31. reinforcement stage

32. reward power

33. situational leadership

34. symposium

35. trait theories of leadership

Chapter 9 Review Questions

These questions are designed to help you understand this chapter's concepts and express your understanding in your own words. For practice with true/false and multiple-choice questions, use the CD-ROM you received with the text.

1. What are the advantages and disadvantages of problem-solving groups? Include the computer-mediated format in your discussion.

2. Identify six basic steps in the rational problem-solving method.

3. Describe characteristics of power important to all group members and the various types of power each member may have.

4. Identify common problems that impede the effectiveness of small groups and suggest ways to minimize these problems.

5. What factors contribute to healthy group cohesiveness?

Chapter 9 Thinking Outside the Box: Synthesizing Your Knowledge

These questions are designed to help you develop the big picture by blending what you've learned in this chapter and elsewhere.

1. What concepts from Chapters 2 could diminish the likelihood of groupthink?

2. Identify specific concepts learned in earlier chapters that would be useful for maintaining positive relationships in groups.

Chapter 9 Answers to Review Questions

1. What are the advantages and disadvantages of problem-solving groups? Include the computer-mediated format in your discussion.

Research shows that groups often produce a larger number of higher-quality solutions than individuals produce because they access greater resources, catch mistakes, and have a greater commitment to the solution if they helped create it. Groups are not advantageous for simple jobs best done by one person, when tasks or people are not interdependent, when there is only one solution, and when there is no chance of disagreement. In computer-mediated groups advantages include ease of scheduling, convenience because of their asynchronous nature with the potential of synchronous "chatting," permanent record of proceedings, and, for some quiet members, more comfort in and more-balanced participation. Disadvantages include a lack of ability to read each others' nonverbal cues, greater time to reach consensus, dropping messages that are too time-consuming to type, and disorganized strings of messages.

2. Identify six basic steps in the rational problem-solving method.

The first step is to identify the problem. Before people begin to talk about solutions and plans, clearly state the group and individual goals. Second, analyze the problem by wording it as a probative question, gather information, and identify impelling and restraining forces (force field analysis). Third, generate large numbers of creative solutions by avoiding criticism, encouraging freewheeling, and piggybacking ideas. Use brainstorming and the nominal group technique to enhance this step of the process. Fourth, evaluate the solutions by determining which are most likely to achieve the desired results with the fewest serious drawbacks. Fifth, implement the plan by identifying specific tasks, necessary resources, individual responsibilities, and backup provisions. Sixth, before heading out, make a plan to follow up and evaluate progress and to structure any necessary revisions.

3. Describe characteristics of power important to all group members and the various types of power each member may have.

All members of groups have the potential to influence others in the group; thus, all members have potential power. Power is not granted only to one person or leader in a group. It is granted by the group in varying degrees to various members. All members can recognize and use their power for the good of the group.

Legitimate (or position) power comes from a title or position: president, TA, treasurer. Coercive power is the ability to impose a punishment on the group and, when used, may generate ill will. The group member who donates the space to meet and threatens to withdraw it if he or she doesn't get something uses coercive power. Not only is this type of power ineffective in achieving group goals, it often results in a negative group climate. Reward power is influence over others that results from offering praise, awards, recognition, or inclusion as well as more-material rewards. Expert power is granted to members whom others believe have special expertise or capabilities the group needs, such as knowledge of a software program or accounting methods. Information power comes not from technical expertise but from knowing how to get something done or knowing who will be helpful. Referent power is granted to group members whom others admire, like, or respect. Others may be influenced by you if they see you as honest, amiable, and trustworthy.

4. Identify common problems that impede the effectiveness of small groups and suggest ways to minimize these problems.

   Four common problems are information underload and overload, unequal participation and pressure to conform. Information underload can be minimized by asking relevant questions and doing adequate formal and informal research. Information overload can be minimized by members' specializing in certain information, selecting and limiting information to relevant and valuable sources rather than bogging down with more information than can be used. Unequal participation is reduced when all members seek to hear from and listen attentively to other members who have relevant contributions, not just those who seek to talk the most. Thanking members for valuable insights and specifically assigning tasks to quieter members can equalize participation, as can the use of nominal groups. To reduce the floor time of overly talkative members, refrain from acknowledging their irrelevant comments or ask directly how a remark is relevant. The problem of groupthink or pressure to conform can be minimized by careful attention to the process of decision making. Be sure all members, regardless of status, have their say and encourage healthy questions and disagreement.

5. What factors contribute to healthy group cohesiveness?

   Groups maintain healthy levels of cohesion by spending time together and expressing positive regard for each other. Productive cohesiveness is high when group members share and make progress toward goals, share norms and values, and refrain from interpersonal threats to each others' status or respectability. Group cohesiveness is stronger when members understand how they are interdependent and see each other as mutually attractive and friendly. Additionally, cohesion increases with more shared experiences and when there is a perception of threats from outside the group.

Chapter 9 Answers to Thinking Outside the Box

1. What concepts from Chapter 2 could diminish the likelihood of groupthink?

    *Groupthink may result from members' falsely assuming that everyone agrees with them and from not listening carefully to outside voices. Therefore, group members would be wise to pay attention to common but inaccurate perceptual tendencies addressed in Chapter 2. Remind group members that we are all susceptible to **self-serving biases.** Look carefully at the **narratives** created in groups and check them against outsiders' narratives. Be aware of the tendency to cling to first impressions and to act without questioning a group's process or solution. In addition, remind group members to guard against the tendency to blame victims and to assume others are similar to themselves. Paying careful attention to these perceptual errors might avoid groupthink. [Boldfaced words are from Chapter 2.]*

2. Identify specific concepts learned in earlier chapters that would be useful for maintaining positive relationships in groups.

    *Building a healthy climate requires respect for other group members. You can build that respect by using **perception checks** and displaying **empathy.** Both demonstrate care and concern for others in your group. Being sensitive to others' **cultures** and their attempts at **impression management** and **facework** can prevent unnecessary misunderstandings and conflicts. [Boldfaced words are from Chapter 2.]*

    *In all group work, **listening** is essential to understand and clarify each person's goals and to convey respect for others. In group work, it is particularly important to be aware of your own and others' listening styles, whether **content oriented, people oriented, action oriented** or **time oriented.** Acknowledging and working with these differences can lead to more-productive relationships. **Informational listening** is vital during each step of the problem-solving method. **Empathic listening** can help group members understand each other better. **Paraphrasing, prompting,** and **supporting** responses can help balance participation. [Boldfaced words are from Chapter 4.]*

CHAPTER 10 CHOOSING AND DEVELOPING A TOPIC

SQ3R in Action

Generate an SQ3R chart for this chapter here: www.teach-nology.com/web_tools/ graphic_org/sq3r/

Survey

Skim the title, Chapter Highlights, objectives ("You should understand" and "You should be able to"), headings, tables, photos, cartoons, figures, charts, and items in the margin. Glance at the titles of the Critical Thinking Probes and Ethical Challenges. At the end of each chapter, look over the list of Key Terms, Activities, and Resources.

Question

Ask yourself questions. What do you know about these topics from your own life experiences and from other classes? Ask these six questions in each section: who, what, when, where, how, and why.

Read

Take one heading at a time and read to find the answers to the questions you've posed.

Recite

In your own words, say the answer aloud and then write it out.

Review

Review each section and then review the whole chapter. This is a good time to use the activities at the end of each chapter and the activities and the sample exams on the CD-ROM. Remember to periodically review the previous chapters as well.

Chapter 10 Outline

(Italicized words are key terms.)

I.   Choosing a topic is an important decision; two guidelines can help.
     A. Look for a topic early.
     B. Choose a topic of interest to you.
II. Defining a general and specific purpose and developing your thesis statement help you develop your speech.
     A. Most speeches have one *general purpose*, although they may overlap.
         1. to entertain
         2. to inform

      3. to persuade
  B. A *purpose statement* helps you focus on the results you want, your *specific purpose*, but is not delivered to the audience.
      1. Purpose statement is receiver oriented.
      2. Purpose statement is specific.
      3. Purpose statement is realistic.
  C. A *thesis statement* summarizes the speech for the audience.
      1. A thesis is the central or main idea of the speech.
      2. A thesis is delivered to the audience.
III. Analyzing the speaking situation is an important step in speech preparation.
  A. *Audience analysis* helps you adapt to your listeners.
      1. Consider your type of audience (passersby, captives, volunteers).
      2. Consider the purpose for the audience to gather.
      3. Consider audience *demographics* (number of people, gender, age, group membership, other factors).
      4. Consider audience attitudes, beliefs, and values.
  B. Analyzing the occasion assists in tailoring your speech to this unique event.
      1. Analyze the time (amount available and relationship to other events).
      2. Analyze the place.
      3. Analyze the audience expectation.
IV. When gathering information, consider several quality sources.
  A. Internet research involves using *search strings* to find Web sites and then evaluating the sites for their credibility, objectivity, and currency.
  B. Library research might involve the use of the library catalog, reference works, periodicals, nonprint materials, *databases,* and librarians.
  C. Interviewing sources can be done in person, by phone, or by e-mail.
  D. Personal observations can provide valuable and interesting information.
  E. *Survey research* uses questionnaires to gather specific information.

Chapter 10 Summary

    Prepare for your speech by completing two activities: choose and develop your topic. The process of choosing a topic proceeds more smoothly if you start early and, once you choose, stay with your topic. Choose a topic that is interesting and familiar to you and one that your audience will find interesting.

    Decide on your general purpose for speaking, whether that is primarily to inform, persuade, or entertain your audience. Next, clarify your specific purpose and write a specific purpose statement that is audience oriented and that clearly and realistically states the outcome you expect. An example is, "After my speech, over half the audience will be able to explain three differences between salsa and mambo." The thesis statement is a one-sentence summary of the central idea, or the main point, of the whole speech. Unlike the specific purpose statement, the thesis is actually spoken to the audience, not just used for your planning. A thesis statement could be, "Three differences between salsa and mambo are rhythm, phrasing, and mood."

You will be more effective as a speaker if you carefully analyze the speaking situation, including both the audience and the occasion. Analyze the type of audience (passersby, captives, and volunteers), its purpose(s) for listening, and its demographics (age, gender, occupation, etc), attitudes, beliefs, and values. Consider these factors as you research and prepare to speak. In analyzing the occasion, ask yourself and others if there are any special considerations with regard to the time and date of your speech, the amount of time allotted for your speech, the location, or audience expectations. For instance, if there has just been a major event in the lives of your audience or the community, you might want to acknowledge or be aware of that.

After you reflect on your own ideas and experiences with your topic, you will need to develop your topic from sources outside yourself. If you use the Internet, understand and utilize search strings to get the most results from search engines. Then evaluate the credibility, currency, and objectivity of the sites. Besides books, the library offers periodicals, reference works, various nonprint items, databases, and librarians to help with your research. When appropriate to your topic, use interviews, observations, and surveys to gather additional information. It is work to gather accurate, thorough, and relevant information on your topic; however, there are ample resources to help you.

Chapter 10 Key Terms

For each of these terms, define the term, give an example, and explain the significance of the term.

1. attitude

2. audience analysis

3. belief

4. database

5. demographics

6. general purpose

7. purpose statement

8. search string

9. specific purpose

10. survey research

11. thesis statement

12. value

Chapter 10 Review Questions

These questions are designed to help you understand this chapter's concepts and express your understanding in your own words. For practice with true/false and multiple-choice questions, use the CD-ROM you received with the text.

1. What are the differences between general purposes, specific purposes, and thesis statements?

2. Why is it important to define your purpose clearly and specifically?

3. Why is it important to analyze a speaking situation?

4. In your own words, describe the most important considerations in choosing an effective topic.

5. Explain several sources that are useful to collecting information for a speech.

Chapter 10 Thinking Outside the Box: Synthesizing Your Knowledge

These questions are designed to help you develop the big picture by blending what you've learned in this chapter and elsewhere.

1. How can the concepts discussed in Chapter 2 with regard to your self-concept and perceptions help you to choose topics for speaking?

2. Discuss three precise ways in which paying attention to principles of language use (Chapter 3) can be used to improve your purpose statement and other speech activities covered in Chapter 10.

Chapter 10 Answers to Review Questions

1. What are the differences between general purposes, specific purposes, and thesis statements?

A general purpose (to inform, persuade, or entertain) is very abstract. It sets the overall goal of a speech but does not give any details. A specific purpose tells specifically and realistically what you hope the audience will know or do after hearing you speak. The thesis statement is the central idea of the speech, the summary of the speech in one sentence.

2. Why is it important to define your purpose clearly and specifically?

Without a clearly defined purpose, it is difficult to focus your remarks, narrow your topic, and stay on track. With a clear purpose, it is easier to decide what support material is important and what organizational pattern will help you achieve your purpose. If you are vague about your purpose, you are more likely to wander off on tangents, and neither you nor the audience will have a clear idea of your goal. You cannot meet your goal if you don't have a clear goal to start.

3. Why is it important to analyze a speaking situation?

    It is important to analyze both parts of a speaking situation, the audience and the occasion, because you can be a more effective speaker if you tailor your remarks to make them meaningful for the particular audience you are speaking to. Knowing who is there and why (audience type and purpose) and understanding the demographics, attitudes, beliefs, and values of the group will help you choose the right level at which to speak and the most relevant information for your speech. Knowing the time, place, and audience expectations can prevent you from making major errors that interfere with the audience's attention. Reference to the unique occasion of your speech can enhance and personalize your speech.

4. In your own words, describe the most important considerations in choosing an effective topic.

    In choosing a topic, be sure to start early so that you have time to research in a variety of ways and thoughtfully plan your speech. Choose a topic that is both interesting to you and to your audience. The better you know your topic, the more confident and knowledgeable you can be.

5. Explain several sources that are useful to collecting information for a speech.

    The Internet, libraries, interviews, personal observation, and surveys are all possible sources of information for speech topics. When using major Internet search engines, be certain that sources are credible, objective and current. Libraries allow you to utilize periodicals, databases, various nonprint materials, and librarians who are trained in research skills.

Chapter 10 Answers to Thinking Outside the Box

1. How can the concepts discussed in Chapter 2 with regard to your self-concept and perceptions help you to choose topics for speaking?

    *The advice in this chapter is to choose a topic you are familiar with and interested in. You can review your writings about your **self-concept**, **self-esteem**, and **impression management** to examine the skills, qualities, values, and goals that are important to you. This can be a source of ideas for speech topics. Explore your **narratives** and the cultural factors that influence your perceptions for further ideas. [Boldfaced words are from Chapter 2.]*

2. Discuss three precise ways in which paying attention to principles of language use (Chapter 3) can be used to improve your purpose statement and other speech activities covered in Chapter 10.

> *You will be more focused if you avoid **equivocal** and **relative** words in your purpose statement and use precise language, such as numbers or percentages ("50 percent of the listeners" rather than "a lot of the listeners"). A purpose statement should be written at a fairly low level on the **abstraction ladder**, so that you think precisely about what you expect to accomplish ("Causes of the 2003 Iraq war" is less abstract than "causes of war"). In describing the demographics of your audience, low-level abstractions can be more meaningful. To know that "40 percent of your audience favors child-care facilities in the workplace" is more meaningful than to know that "a lot of the audience favors child-care facilities in the workplace." Avoid **slang** and **jargon** so that your thoughts are more clearly expressed with regard to your purpose. If someone is describing special constraints with regard to the time or room you'll be speaking in, be certain you use a perception check, particularly for any **equivocal** or **abstract** words. "We'll fit you in between two other speakers" is abstract. You could ask what this means. At precisely what time? How much time? What will the audience's perception of you be? [Boldfaced words are from Chapter 3.]*

CHAPTER 11 ORGANIZATION AND SUPPORT

SQ3R in Action

Generate an SQ3R chart for this chapter here: www.teach-nology.com/web_tools/ graphic_org/sq3r/

Survey

Skim the title, Chapter Highlights, objectives ("You should understand" and "You should be able to"), headings, tables, photos, cartoons, figures, charts, and items in the margin. Glance at the titles of the Critical Thinking Probes and Ethical Challenges. At the end of each chapter, look over the list of Key Terms, Activities, and Resources.

Question

Ask yourself questions. What do you know about these topics from your own life experiences and from other classes? Ask these six questions in each section: who, what, when, where, how, and why.

Read

Take one heading at a time and read to find the answers to the questions you've posed.

Recite

In your own words, say the answer aloud and then write it out.

Review

Review each section and then review the whole chapter. This is a good time to use the activities at the end of each chapter and the activities and the sample exams on the CD-ROM. Remember to periodically review the previous chapters as well.

Chapter 11 Outline

(Italicized words are key terms.)

I. Understand and use *working outlines, formal outlines*, and speaking notes to help you set up your *basic speech structure* more effectively.

II. Apply outlining principles regarding standard symbols and formats and the rules of division and parallel wording.

    A. Use standard symbols and formats such as the use of Roman numerals for main points, capital letters for subpoints, and standard numbers for sub-subpoints, each indented under the other.

B. Apply the rules of division (each division has at least two points) and parallel wording within divisions.

III. Choose one of these logical organization *patterns* that is right for your topic and purpose: *time (climax), space, topic, problem–solution, cause–effect,* or *motivated sequence.*

IV. *Transitions* review past ideas and preview upcoming main points to give your audience a clear idea of how parts of the speech relate to each other.

V. Effective beginnings and endings add to your effectiveness as a speaker.

    A. *Introductions* must gain your audience's attention, preview main points, set the tone, and show the topic's importance.

    B. Gain attention in one of these ways: refer to the audience, occasion, relationship of audience and subject, or something familiar; use an interesting fact or question; or tell an appropriate anecdote, quotation, or joke.

    C. Use your *conclusion* to summarize with a review of your thesis and main points and provide a memorable ending.

    D. Avoid abrupt endings, rambling, introducing new points, or apologizing in your conclusion.

VI. Supporting materials are vital to the development of your speech.

    A. Supporting materials function to clarify main points, provide proof of your main points, and make your speech memorable and interesting.

    B. Select appropriate and varied supporting material such as definitions, *examples* (both factual and *hypothetical*), *statistics, analogies* or compare–contrasts, *anecdotes,* quotations, and *testimonies.*

    C. Choose one of two styles to present supporting material: *narration* or *citation.*

VII. Use *visual aids* to support or illustrate your ideas by providing evidence of a point, or showing what something looks like, how something works, or how things relate to each other.

    D. Choose from these types of visual aids: objects and models, diagrams, word charts, number charts, pie charts, bar charts, column charts, and line charts.

    E. Choose from these types of media: chalkboards, white boards, polymer surfaces, flip pads/poster boards, handouts, projectors, and other electronic media.

    F. Follow these rules for successful use of visual aids:

        1. Keep the visual aid simple.

        2. Make the size large enough so all audience members can see it.

        3. Make visual aids visually interesting.

        4. Keep visual aids appropriate for you, your audience, and the occasion and relevant to the point you are making.

        5. Make sure the visual aid will work properly when you need it.

Chapter 11 Summary

A good speech is built using the basic speech structure of introduction, body, and conclusion. This structure shows the relationship of ideas to your thesis and to each other. It also helps the audience follow and remember your main points. A working outline is an ongoing, fluid document used by a speaker to create a rough draft of a speech. A formal outline may be used as a visual aid or a record of a speech or for speech analysis. Formal outlines used in speech classes usually require a bibliography. Like the working outline, speaking notes are generally on cards that you take to the podium or hold in your hands and are for your use only. There are many styles and forms of speaking notes that work well.

Outlines are most effective when they follow principles of outlining with regard to standard symbols, format, division, and parallel wording. Organization is visually clearer with the uniform use of symbols and indentations of similar levels of ideas. Three to five main ideas are common; each idea must be divided into at least two parts if it is divided at all. Using parallel words for parallel levels of ideas adds clarity to the speech.

Common patterns of organization for speeches include time (climax), space, topic, problem–solution, cause–effect, and motivated sequence. Time patterns show the chronology of events that did or will take place. Variations on the time pattern include the climax pattern that builds suspense and the reverse, an anticlimactic pattern, often used when a speaker needs to gain interest and attention at the outset. Space patterns organize ideas according to the physical areas, proximity, or direction. Topic patterns use categories that may be original or very well established. The problem–solution pattern, like its name, uses two main divisions: the problem and the solution. The cause–effect pattern may have just those two divisions or add a third, a solution, as well. Another pattern, the motivated sequence, has five divisions: attention, need, satisfaction, visualization, and action steps.

Transitions help create a smooth-flowing speech as they link past and future points together and show their correlation to each other. Internal previews and internal reviews help listeners look forward and backward in the speech and remember the sequence of thoughts.

The first and last impressions an audience receives are so important that a speaker must pay special attention to the introduction and conclusion of a speech. An introduction captures attention, previews main points, sets the mood and tone for the speaker, and demonstrates the topic's importance. The best-known ways to gain attention include references to the audience, the occasion, the relationship of the audience and the topic, or something familiar to the audience. Other methods include using unusual or startling facts, questions, anecdotes, quotations, or appropriate humor.

An effective conclusion reviews the thesis and the main points and creates a memorable ending. Effective speakers avoid the common mistakes of ending too abruptly, rambling at the end, introducing new points, or apologizing.

Speeches need credible and effective supporting material to clarify or prove the points made, to spark interest, and to make them memorable. Use a variety of relevant and appropriate supporting materials including definitions, descriptions, analogies, anecdotes, examples (both real and hypothetical), statistics, quotations, and testimonies. Supporting material can be presented in one of two ways by a speaker: narration or citation. Narration creates more drama and storylike qualities for the audience. Citations state the information more directly.

Visual aids are graphic devices used to illustrate or support ideas in a presentation. Their purpose may be to serve as evidence or to show how things look, work, or relate to each other. The types of visual aids available to speakers are vast: objects and models, diagrams, word charts, number charts, pie charts, bar charts, column charts, and line charts.

In addition to knowing what visual aids to use, the speaker has many choices of media for presenting visual aids. Choices include chalkboards, white boards, polymer surfaces, flip pads, poster boards, handouts, projectors, and electronic media, including PowerPoint. Presenters need to be aware of the pros and cons of using all media, including PowerPoint, to make a wise choice for a given occasion and audience.

Following reliable guidelines for visual aids enhances their effectiveness. Keep the visuals relatively simple and attractive. Use sizes that are visible to all audience members. Be sure the visuals are appropriate and closely related to the speech itself, and be certain your visuals are dependable.

Understanding these principles of organization and support can give you greater understanding and clarity about the ideas you are presenting to your audience and can give your audience better comprehension and recollection of your main points.

Chapter 11 Key Terms

For each of these terms, define the term, give an example, and explain the significance of the term.

1. analogies

2. anecdote

3. bar charts

4. basic speech structure

5. cause–effect patterns

6. citation

7. climax patterns

8. column charts

9. conclusion (of a speech)

10. diagram

11. example

12. formal outline

13. hypothetical examples

14. introduction (of a speech)

15. line chart

16. models

17. motivated sequence

18. narration

19. number charts

20. pie charts

21. problem–solution pattern

22. space pattern

23. statistics

24. testimony

25. time pattern

26. topic pattern

27. transitions

28. visual aids

29. word charts

30. working outline

Chapter 11 Review Questions

These questions are designed to help you understand this chapter's concepts and express your understanding in your own words. For practice with true/false and multiple-choice questions, use the CD-ROM you received with the text.

1. Show how the basic structure of a speech helps to organize a speech. Explain the importance of clear speech organization.

2. What are the basic steps in organizing a speech?

3. Explain the functions and importance of introductions, conclusions, and transitions.

4. What are some basic functions and types of supporting materials?

5. What principles guide a speaker to choose visual aids effectively?

Chapter 11 Thinking Outside the Box: Synthesizing Your Knowledge

These questions are designed to help you develop the big picture by blending what you've learned in this chapter and elsewhere.

1. What principles of perception (Chapter 2) have implications for speakers regarding introductions and conclusions?

2. How could information on nonverbal communication (Chapter 5) assist the speaker in applying the principles for choosing and using visual aids effectively?

Chapter 11 Answers to Review Questions

1. Show how the basic structure of a speech helps to organize a speech. Explain the importance of clear speech organization.

The basic structure of a speech includes an introduction to let the audience know the thesis and get them interested in the topic. The second part, 80 percemt of the speech, is the body. This is a development of the thesis with supporting material. The third part is the conclusion reminding the audience of your thesis and main points and providing a memorable ending. The introduction and conclusion together usually comprise no more than 20 percent of the speech. These parts are important to get and keep an audience's attention, develop your main ideas with credible and relevant support, and provide a review and bring closure to your main points. Good organization helps you clarify your own thinking and, thus, helps the audience comprehend and remember your ideas.

2. What are the basic steps in organizing a speech?

Begin with your goal and your thesis. As you research your ideas, consider the most logical organizational pattern for your ideas. You will probably reorganize your ideas several times and do more research while preparing your working outline. When you settle on your thesis and organize your main points, you'll organize your supporting material for greatest effect. Then, you can create your transitions to help the audience follow your organization and ideas. Now you'll write your introduction, conclusion, and the transitions between the body of the speech and the beginning and ending. Finally, you will create a formal outline and construct your bibliography.

3. Explain the importance and functions of introductions, conclusions, and transitions.

    An introduction is most important because it is your first, and perhaps only, opportunity to get your audience's attention and interest and convince them the topic is important to them. It is possible to get and keep their attention if you do it initially. If you lose this chance, it is extremely difficult to get their attention back. So doing this right initially is important. Additionally, the introduction aids comprehension by previewing your key points and setting the tenor for the rest of the speech, so your audience is clear about what to listen for.

    An effective conclusion reviews your thesis and key points and creates a memorable finale for your audience. If you end abruptly, ramble on and on, introduce new points, or apologize, you lessen the effectiveness of your final impression.

    Transitions are vital to help an audience see the connections between the introduction and the body, the main points, and the body and the conclusion. Transitions show and remind the audience of the design and structure of the speech, and they help pull the speech together and create an impression of a unified and well-organized whole.

4. What are some basic functions of and types of supporting materials?

    Supporting materials clarify the points you make in your speech, add interest to those points, convince an audience that your points are valid, and help an audience remember your ideas. The types of supporting materials that can help do this include definitions, descriptions, analogies, anecdotes, examples, statistics, quotations, and testimony.

5. What principles guide a speaker to choose visual aids effectively?

    A speaker will always choose ethically and wisely those visual aids that help an audience understand the evidence for points he's making (seeing the chart showing the gap in wages), what something looks like (a building or part of town or a city), how something functions (how the jaw performs or the endocrine system operates), and how different things relate to each other (how Social Security benefits relate to inflation).

    The best choices are those that favor simplicity over complexity in both design and language, attractiveness and neatness over messiness and disorganization, appropriateness to the audience and topic over offensive or unsuitable items, and reliability of the medium over guesswork or nerve-wracking unknowns.

Chapter 11 Answers to Thinking Outside the Box

1. What principles of perception (Chapter 2) have implications for speakers regarding introductions and conclusions?

*One perceptual tendency for speakers to be aware of is that most people will **cling to first impressions** even if they're wrong. The implication of this for speakers is that introductions take on even greater importance. Knowing that people will make judgments about you, your topic, and your credibility initially tells you to carefully prepare and practice introductions. Another common perceptual tendency to be aware of (even if it is inaccurate) is that most **people assume others are similar to themselves**. A possible implication of this is that if audience members didn't understand your main points, they'll assume not just that they missed something, but that others didn't understand either. So, as a speaker, you want to be sure that your introductions and conclusions are very clear so your audience members will understand (and then they can assume that you were perfectly clear to others as well). [Boldfaced phrases are false assumptions discussed in Chapter 2.]*

2. How could information on nonverbal communication (Chapter 5) assist the speaker in applying the principles for choosing and using visual aids effectively?

*Chapter 5's discussion with regard to the functions of nonverbal communication can be applied to choosing and using visual aids. If the visual aids are considered nonverbal communication, the speaker can then consider what function he or she wants these visuals to play. According to Chapter 5, nonverbal communication can **repeat** what is said verbally. Often the visual will accurately do this. A speaker would want to be careful that the visual never **contradicts** what is being said verbally. Visually aids may at times, for dramatic effect, **substitute** for words. An example might be a speaker talking about Very Special Arts and the artwork produced by students with various disabilities. To illustrate a point, that the artwork is exceptional, the speaker might be silent and merely display a piece of work. Often visual aids will **complement** what is said verbally, as diagrams and charts often do. [Boldfaced words are functions of nonverbal communication discussed in Chapter 5.]*

CHAPTER 12 PRESENTING YOUR MESSAGE

SQ3R in Action

Generate an SQ3R chart for this chapter here: www.teach-nology.com/web_tools/ graphic_org/sq3r/

Survey

Skim the title, Chapter Highlights, objectives ("You should understand" and "You should be able to"), headings, tables, photos, cartoons, figures, charts, and items in the margin. Glance at the titles of the Critical Thinking Probes and Ethical Challenges. At the end of each chapter, look over the list of Key Terms, Activities, and Resources.

Question

Ask yourself questions. What do you know about these topics from your own life experiences and from other classes? Ask these six questions in each section: who, what, when, where, how, and why.

Read

Take one heading at a time and read to find the answers to the questions you've posed.

Recite

In your own words, say the answer aloud and then write it out.

Review

Review each section and then review the whole chapter. This is a good time to use the activities at the end of each chapter and the activities and the sample exams on the CD-ROM. Remember to periodically review the previous chapters as well.

Chapter 12 Outline

(Italicized words are key terms.)

I. You can use specific techniques to manage *debilitative stage fright* if you understand its sources and the how it differs from *facilitative stage fright*.
   A. Stage fright that energizes speakers can be facilitative, but that which prevents clear thinking and leads to fumbling and mistakes is debilitative.
   B. Debilitative stage fright often comes from prior negative experiences or from irrational thinking, such as the *fallacies of catastrophic failure, perfection, approval,* or *overgeneralization.*
   C. Speakers can minimize or overcome debilitative stage fright with several

techniques.

    1. Use the energy from nervousness to add enthusiasm to your speech.

    2. Be rational about your fears.

    3. Maintain a receiver orientation.

    4. Use affirmations and *visualizations* to maintain a positive attitude.

    5. Be prepared.

II. Choose the type of delivery that has the most advantages for your speaking situation.

    A. *Extemporaneous speech* is planned but not memorized and is the most common type of speech.

    B. *Impromptu speech* is given without any or much preparation time, speaking off the cuff.

    C. A *manuscript speeches* is read, usually because of time constraints or the absolute need for accuracy.

    D. A *memorized speech* often appears less effective and very formal.

III. Practice your speech by one or more of these methods: talk through it, tape record it (audio or video), speak to real people, and speak in the real setting.

IV. Follow visual and verbal guidelines for delivery to enhance your effectiveness.

    A. Pay attention to the visual aspects of delivery such as appearance, movement, posture, facial expression, and eye contact.

    B. Recognize and use effective auditory aspects of delivery such as volume, *rate*, *pitch*, and *articulation* (avoiding problems of *deletion, substitution, addition,* and *slurring*).

V. Offer constructive criticism to classmates by being both positive and substantive.

Chapter 12 Summary

Assuming you've followed the steps for preparing, organizing, and developing your message, your next focus will be on how to best deliver it.

Facilitative stage fright (also called communication apprehension or anxiety) can improve speech performance by creating energy and facilitating quick thinking. If stage fright impedes performance so the speaker isn't functioning and speaking intelligibly, the stage fright has become debilitative. Previous negative experiences or irrational thinking cause debilitative stage fright. Fallacies, or false thinking, include the fallacy of catastrophic failure (thinking the worst will happen), the fallacy of perfection (believing you're not okay if you're human and not perfect), the fallacy of approval (believing everyone must approve of all you say and do), and the fallacy of overgeneralization (overreacting and characterizing minor things as always and never). Try different ways to overcome stage fright: use your energy (nervousness) to produce enthusiasm, think rationally about your fear, become receiver- or audience-oriented, adopt and maintain a positive attitude with affirmations and/or visualizations, and be prepared.

Speeches are generally delivered in one of four ways: extemporaneous, impromptu, manuscript, or memorized. Each has advantages and disadvantages. An extemporaneous speech is carefully prepared, then delivered spontaneously in a conversational manner. This oft-used delivery technique allows speakers to use brief notes and maintain touch with the audiences. It is rarely exact in wording, time, or grammar. An impromptu speech is given without advance preparation. A speaker can wisely use the short time between being called on and starting to speak to organize one's thoughts. Impromptu speeches can be very original, responsive to others, and brief. A manuscript speech is read word-for-word and works well for precisely timed or carefully recorded contexts. A memorized speech may lack spontaneity and naturalness and be less effective. However, in order not to lose the whole opportunity, a speaker who must use a memorized format is advised to practice, practice, practice.

Regardless of the type of delivery chosen or dictated by the situation, all speeches benefit from a delivery that sounds smooth and natural. This comes from practice. One technique to aid your rehearsal is to talk through the speech to yourself, actually saying everything you intend to say in the real presentation. A second technique is to tape record or videotape yourself and see what you actually sound and look like. A third technique is to gather a group of friends or family together to be your "audience" and speak to them. A final technique is to present the speech to at least one person in the room that you will actually be speaking in.

Effective delivery necessitates your effective use of both visual and auditory guidelines. Visual aspects of delivery include your appearance, movement, posture, facial expression, and eye contact. Match your appearance to the audience's expectations. Your movement, if voluntary, adds meaning to your speech and a relaxed yet straight posture lets you connect to audiences in a positive way. Your facial expressions can demonstrate sincerity and interest to your audience. Perhaps most important of all, connect with your audience through eye contact. Look at each person briefly rather than trying to sweep them all in without really connecting with anyone, and use your eye contact to see how the audience is responding to you.

Effective use of the auditory aspects of delivery enhances your speech so use your volume, rate, pitch, and articulation to your advantage. Your volume must be loud enough to be heard, but not too loud for the room or for the size of the group. Rate and pitch can be effectively used for emphasis and interest. You can slow down to call attention to important words, phrases or ideas. A downward pitch sounds authoritative. Avoid common articulation mistakes that interfere with your audience's comprehension of your ideas such as deletion (leaving out sounds), substitution (using incorrect sounds), addition (adding incorrect syllables or sounds), and slurring (blurring words together so they are not understood).

While delivering speeches in class, you may be called upon to critique classmates' presentations. When done well, constructive criticism among classmates benefits everyone, and there is collaborative learning. When asked to critique a classmate, begin by pointing out what the speaker did well. You can follow this with what you believe can be improved, telling specifically how it can be improved. Use "I" statements rather than "you" statements to offer your opinion: "I couldn't hear you," rather than, "You didn't speak loud enough." Be specific and positive in your appraisal of your classmates.

Chapter 12 Key Terms

For each of these terms, define the term, give an example, and explain the significance of the term.

1. addition

2. articulation

3. debilitative stage fright

4. deletion

5. extemporaneous speech

6. facilitative stage fright

7. fallacy of approval

8. fallacy of catastrophic failure

9. fallacy of overgeneralization

10. fallacy of perfection

11. impromptu speech

12. irrational thinking

13. manuscript speeches

14. memorized speeches

15. pitch

16. rate

17. slurring

18. substitution

19. visualization

Chapter 12 Review Questions

These questions are designed to help you understand this chapter's concepts and express your understanding in your own words. For practice with true/false and multiple-choice questions, use the CD-ROM you received with the text.

1. Distinguish among these types of delivery: extemporaneous, impromptu, manuscript, and memorized. Give examples of when you might use each.

2. Describe some effective practice techniques.

3. Identify visual and auditory aspects of speech delivery.

4. What are some sources of debilitative stage fright? How can a speaker overcome debilitative stage fright?

Chapter 12 Thinking Outside the Box: Synthesizing Your Knowledge

These questions are designed to help you develop the big picture by blending what you've learned in this chapter and elsewhere.

1. How can the concepts from Chapter 7 on improving relationships help you be more effective in critiquing your classmates?

2. Discuss three precise ways in which paying attention to principles of language use (Chapter 3) can be used to improve your understanding of the context of your speech.

Chapter 12 Answers to Review Questions

1. Distinguish among these types of delivery: extemporaneous, impromptu, manuscript, and memorized. Give examples of when you might use each.

Extemporaneous speeches are the type required in most speech classes; they are well planned, organized, researched, and rehearsed, but each time one is presented it is with slightly different language. It is not memorized or read. An impromptu speech is unscheduled and unrehearsed. Such a speech would be used when you are called to speak at a PTA meeting or when you decide to speak up at a town hall meeting. You are speaking from neither prepared notes nor memory, but still trying to be organized. A manuscript speech would be used when timing must be exact, as in a Public Service announcement for a one-minute radio spot. You would read the exact words so that the timing and accuracy are precise. A memorized speech might be used for a short toast at a wedding. This is probably the least used type of delivery because the potential for forgetting is great.

2. Describe some effective practice techniques.

One effective way to practice is to create a real audience. Gather a few people and give your speech to them, treating them as your real audience. Another way to practice is to go to the place where you will be speaking and practice in the location with at least one person to speak to in order to get a feel for that space. Without real people or the real location, it is still beneficial to talk through your speech. Don't just look at your notes or outline and don't just say it in your head, give the whole speech out loud to help you format the words, phrasing, and timing. One other way to practice is to use technology: videotape or audio tape yourself and then watch and/or listen to yourself to see what works well and what can be improved.

3. Identify visual and auditory aspects of speech delivery.

Consider various aspects of visual and auditory delivery. First, consider your appearance; be sure that you understand the audience's expectations and dress accordingly. Businesslike appearances often aid your credibility. Movement can indicate confidence and enthusiasm. If you are purposeful in your movements, you can add meaning and emphasis to your delivery. Your posture should be relaxed yet attentive. Too much slouching or relaxation makes you appear uninteresting or lacking in credibility. Too much rigidity looks too formal, too nervous, or too controlled. Facial expressions reflect your sincerity and involvement with your message. Eye contact increases your immediacy with the audience and indicates interest and involvement. Lack of eye contact can make you seem uncaring, uninterested, unknowledgeable, or insincere. The first important auditory aspect of delivery is volume; you need enough volume to be heard and to sound sincere and credible. Speaking too slowly can lead to your being perceived as dull; speak too fast, and you may not be understood. Pitch is important, especially at the end of sentences. A raised pitch sounds insincere or lacking in knowledge or credibility. A dropped pitch at the end lends you an air of credibility and authority. Finally, articulation can add to the perception of credibility; failure to articulate words accurately can diminish your credibility and understandability.

4. What are some sources of debilitative stage fright? How can a speaker overcome debilitative stage fright?

Debilitative stage fright often comes from previous bad experiences or irrational thinking or fallacies. Previous bad experiences need to be recognized as that: previous experiences. They can be acknowledged as such but need not be repeated in the current situation. Irrational thinking often falls into one of four types of fallacies: catastrophic failure, perfection, approval, or overgeneralization. For each type of irrational thinking, the speaker can replace the irrational fallacy with more-accurate thinking. Instead of dwelling on what could go wrong, remind yourself that the worst will probably not happen. Instead of believing you must be flawless to be okay, remind yourself that audiences don't expect perfection. Instead of thinking that everyone must approve of everything, remind yourself that you don't need to please everyone all of the time. And instead of overgeneralizing (always, never), be more accurate (sometimes, once in a while, twice).

Chapter 12 Answers to Thinking Outside the Box

1. How can the concepts from Chapter 7 on improving relationships help you be more effective in critiquing your classmates?

*When you are placed in the role of critiquing your classmates, you may have some discomfort with the role. However, the term "critic" needn't have a negative connotation. Think of yourself as being helpful to your classmates, like a coach, assisting them in focusing on their strengths as well as areas that could be improved. Often, describing what you saw and felt is helpful, as your perspective is different from the speaker's. Chapter 7 described **Gibb categories** of characteristics which promote **communication climates** that might be either defensive or supportive. In critiquing your classmates, you will want to be perceived as supportive and contributing to a supportive classroom climate. You don't want your classmates to become defensive and unable to benefit from your remarks. According to Gibb, this means you would want to be perceived as **descriptive** rather than **evaluative,** and you can do this best by using "I" statements rather than "you" statements and using concrete, factual language rather than emotive, judgmental language. It would be better to say, "I didn't hear any support for your second point," rather than, "You totally blew off your second point." According to Gibb, you'll also create a more supportive climate and generate less defensiveness if you strive to portray **empathy** not **neutrality**, **equality** not **superiority**, **spontaneity** not manipulation or **strategy**, **provisionalism** not **certainty**, and **problem orientation** not **controlling messages**. Remember, there is less defensiveness when a person believes the evaluation given is appropriate for the context. [Boldfaced words are from Chapter 7.]*

2. Discuss three precise ways in which paying attention to principles of language use (Chapter 3) can be used to improve your understanding of the context of your speech.

> *When planning for your presentation, you'll want to know precisely where and when you'll be speaking. If someone is describing special constraints with regard to the time or room you'll be speaking in, be certain you use a perception check or more-specific language, particularly for any **equivocal** or **abstract** words. If you're told, "We'll have an in-focus projector and microphone available for you," recognize that the statement is abstract. With regard to the projector, ask, What kind? What year? Is it compatible with your laptop? "Microphone" is also abstract: What kind? Will it require clothing with a collar? Will it require you to stay in one spot? If you're told, "We'll fit you in between two other speakers," you might want to ask at what time, and how many minutes you'll have. You could use a perception check, "When you say you'll fit me in, do you mean that I'll have less time than the others or that each speaker will be asked to be shorter?" [Boldfaced words are from Chapter 3.]*

CHAPTER 13 INFORMATIVE SPEAKING

SQ3R in Action

Generate an SQ3R chart for this chapter here: www.teach-nology.com/web_tools/ graphic_org/sq3r/

Survey

Skim the title, Chapter Highlights, objectives ("You should understand" and "You should be able to"), headings, tables, photos, cartoons, figures, charts, and items in the margin. Glance at the titles of the Critical Thinking Probes and Ethical Challenges. At the end of each chapter, look over the list of Key Terms, Activities, and Resources.

Question

Ask yourself questions. What do you know about these topics from your own life experiences and from other classes? Ask these six questions in each section: who, what, when, where, how, and why.

Read

Take one heading at a time and read to find the answers to the questions you've posed.

Recite

In your own words, say the answer aloud and then write it out.

Review

Review each section and then review the whole chapter. This is a good time to use the activities at the end of each chapter and the activities and the sample exams on the CD-ROM. Remember to periodically review the previous chapters as well.

Chapter 13 Outline

(Italicized words are key terms.)

I. Categorizing types of informative speaking
   A. Some informative speeches are defined by their content, which might focus on objects, processes, events, or concepts.
   B. Other informative speeches are defined by their purposes, which might be *descriptions, explanations, or instructions.*

II. Informative versus persuasive topics
    A. Informative topics tend to be noncontroversial.
    B. Informative speaking is not intended to change audience attitudes.
III. Techniques of informative speaking
    A. Define a specific informative purpose by writing an *informative purpose statement* and a clear thesis.
    B. Create *information hunger* by emphasizing how the topic relates to audience needs, such as physical, identity, social, or practical needs.
    C. Make your speech easy to listen to by limiting the amount of information, by using what is familiar to lead to the unfamiliar, and by using what is simple to lead to the complex.
    D. Emphasize important points by using repetition and *signposts*.
    E. Use a clear organization and structure.
        1. Begin with an interesting introduction.
        2. Structure the body of the speech with a clear organizational plan, internal summaries, reviews, and transitions.
        3. Create a conclusion that reviews your main points and brings closure.
    F. Use supporting material effectively with *vocal citations*.
    G. Use clear language that includes precise vocabulary and simple syntax.
    H. Generate *audience involvement*.
        1. Personalize your speech.
        2. Use *audience participation*.
        3. Ask for volunteers.
        4. Conduct a question-and-answer period in which you focus on substantive issues, paraphrase questions, avoid defensiveness, and answer briefly.

Chapter 13 Summary

Informative speeches can be classified by content or purpose. Those classified by content include speeches about objects (the Sears Tower), processes (spread of a computer virus), events (the 1929 stock market crash), and concepts (ageism). Speeches classified by purpose include descriptions that tell "what," explanations that answer "why," or instructions that tell "how." Examples of such speeches, respectively, could describe what a human resources manager does, explain why some organizations use stress interviews to select new employees, or give instructions on how to prepare for a job interview.

Informative speeches differ from persuasive speeches in two ways: informative topics tend to be noncontroversial, and informative speakers are not focused on changing audience attitudes.

So how can an informative speaker be most effective? Eight techniques can help. Before structuring a speech, first clearly define a specific informative purpose that is audience centered, exact, and realistic. State what the audience will know or be able to do at the conclusion of your speech, for instance, "The audience will be able to list three methods to save money on credit cards." Second, make the audience want to listen by relating the speech to the audience's needs (physical, identity, social, practical), not to your needs. Third, make it easy for your audience to listen by restricting the amount of information presented, using familiar and simpler concepts to lead to an understanding of less-familiar and more-complex ideas.

Fourth, as you actually speak, emphasize your important points for the audience by repeating the main points and using signposts ("Now, this is the key point . . .") to clue your audience to especially important concepts. Fifth, it is essential to organize and structure your speech in this way: Carefully arrange no more than three to five main points, tying them together with transitions, internal summaries and previews, and a strong introduction (preview) and conclusion (review).

Sixth, use thoughtfully chosen verbal and visual material to support your main points and use vocal citations to identify your sources. Seventh, use clear and simple language by avoiding jargon, choosing precise words, and speaking in short, direct sentences. One final technique for effective informative speeches is to generate audience involvement in one of several ways: personalize your speech, get audience members to participate in an activity, use volunteers, or open up a question-and-answer period.

Chapter 13 Key Terms

For each of these terms, define the term, give an example, and explain the significance of the term.

1. audience involvement

2. audience participation

3. description

4. explanations

5. information anxiety

6. information hunger

7. information overload

8. informative purpose statement

9. instructions

10. knowledge

11. signposts

12. vocal citations

Chapter 13 Review Questions

These questions are designed to help you understand this chapter's concepts and express your understanding in your own words. For practice with true/false and multiple-choice questions, use the CD-ROM you received with the text.

1. What are two subcategories of informative speeches that are related to content? Related to purpose?

2. In what two ways is an informative speech different from a persuasive speech?

3. Why is it important to create information hunger in an informative speech?

4. In your own words, describe the most important steps in organizing your speech and using supporting material.

5. Explain two techniques to emphasize the important points of your speech.

6. Describe four ways that you can generate audience involvement, and list advantages and disadvantages of using each.

Chapter 13 Thinking Outside the Box: Synthesizing Your Knowledge

· These questions are designed to help you develop the big picture by blending what you've learned in this chapter and elsewhere.

1. How can the way you define your specific purpose increase or decrease your perception of your stage fright (Chapter 12) and your means of overcoming it?

2. Describe how you can use the functions of communication (Chapter 1) to create information hunger. Use specific topics to give examples.

Chapter 13 Answers to Review Questions

1. What are two subcategories of informative speeches that are related to content? Related to purpose?

Speeches classified by content include speeches about objects, processes, events, and concepts. Speeches classified by purpose include descriptions, explanations, and instructions.

2. In what two ways is an informative speech different from a persuasive speech?

Informative speeches differ from persuasive speeches in two ways: informative topics tend to be noncontroversial, and informative speakers are not focused on changing audience attitudes.

3. Why is it important to create information hunger in an informative speech?

    The audience needs a reason to listen that is related to their own needs and desires. If the topic is important to you but not to your audience, they aren't motivated to listen. Use their own needs (physical, identity, social, and practical) to create information hunger.

4. In your own words, describe the most important steps in organizing your speech and using supporting material.

    Begin with a clear informative purpose. Divide your topic into three to five main points and carefully order them. Create a strong introduction to preview the speech and a strong conclusion to review key points. Provide continuity and cohesion by using transitions, internal summaries, and internal previews to make your points understood.

    Use verbal and visual material to effectively support your main points and use vocal citations to state the source of your information.

5. Explain two techniques to emphasize the important points of your speech.

    Emphasize your important points for the audience by using repetition of the main points and using signposts ("Now, this is the key point . . .") to clue your audience to especially important concepts.

6. Describe four ways that you can generate audience involvement and list advantages and disadvantages of using each.

Method	Advantages	Disadvantages
1. *Use personal references.*	*The audience sees you as a person—not an impersonal speaker.*	*Your credibility may be lowered if your personal references are resented by the audience or clearly indicate less expertise than the audience expects.*
2. *Get audience members to participate.*	*All members are involved: filling in a form, raising a hand, voting.*	*Poorly chosen participatory opportunities may create resentment and distract from your message.*
3. *Use audience volunteers.*	*Creates interest from all members; volunteers are especially involved.*	*If the exercise does not make a point or is not relevant to the speech, audiences may disapprove.*

Method	Advantages	Disadvantages
4. Hold a Q&A session.	Audience can be as involved as they like; unclear points can be clarified.	Your credibility is lowered if you don't know answers that an audience believes you should or if you pretend to know what you don't.

Chapter 13 Answers to Thinking Outside the Box

1. How can the way you define your specific purpose increase or decrease your perception of your stage fright (Chapter 12) and your means of overcoming it?

Creating a realistic purpose statement that you feel confident about can help you have less debilitative stage fright. The fallacy of perfection is less apt to affect you if your specific purpose is realistic ("Half the audience will . . ." rather than, "ALL of the audience will . . ."). Specificity in your purpose can help reduce the fallacy of overgeneralization because you will be clear in your mind about what you want to accomplish with your speech and less apt to fall prey to mental talk like, "I'll never be able to get the audience to understand . . ." (some vague and abstract idea).

2. Describe how you can use the functions of communication (Chapter 1) to create information hunger. Use specific topics to give examples.

Chapter 1 explains that the reason we spend so much time communicating is to fulfill our physical, identity, social, and practical needs. In preparing an informative speech, the speaker can create information hunger by helping the audience to see how the speech can function to fulfill these needs. For example, create information hunger regarding physical needs with speeches about maintaining health or getting scholarships. Speeches that help us understand who we are and who we can become can meet identity needs. Speeches about networking, friendships, and being assertive can meet the social needs of the audience, and many speeches can help us achieve practical goals (how to fix a car, invest in bonds, back up your hard drive).

CHAPTER 14 PERSUASIVE SPEAKING

SQ3R in Action

Generate an SQ3R chart for this chapter here: www.teach-nology.com/web_tools/ graphic_org/sq3r/

Survey

Skim the title, Chapter Highlights, objectives ("You should understand" and "You should be able to"), headings, tables, photos, cartoons, figures, charts, and items in the margin. Glance at the titles of the Critical Thinking Probes and Ethical Challenges. At the end of each chapter, look over the list of Key Terms, Activities, and Resources.

Question

Ask yourself questions. What do you know about these topics from your own life experiences and from other classes? Ask these six questions in each section: who, what, when, where, how, and why.

Read

Take one heading at a time and read to find the answers to the questions you've posed.

Recite

In your own words, say the answer aloud and then write it out.

Review

Review each section and then review the whole chapter. This is a good time to use the activities at the end of each chapter and the activities and the sample exams on the CD-ROM. Remember to periodically review the previous chapters as well.

Chapter 14 Outline

(Italicized words are key terms.)

I. *Persuasion* is usually incremental, interactive, and ethical.
   A. Persuasion does not involve coercion.
   B. *Social judgment theory* explains that persuasion takes place incrementally and can be understood by acknowledging a person's *anchor*, *latitude of acceptance*, *latitude of rejection*, and *latitude of noncommitment*.
   C. Persuasion is interactive.
   D. *Ethical persuasion* is in the audience's best interest and is not false or misleading.

II. Persuasive messages can be characterized in three ways: by types of propositions, by desired outcomes, or by directness of approach.

    A. Propositions are one of three types: *propositions of fact, value,* or *policy.*

    B. When persuasion is characterized by the desired outcome, messages might be to *convince* the audience of something or to *actuate* the audience (move them to begin or discontinue an action).

    C. Persuasion can also be categorized into *direct persuasion* or *indirect persuasion.*

III. Important steps to create persuasive messages include setting clear purposes, structuring clear messages, using solid evidence, and avoiding fallacies.

    A. Set a clear, persuasive purpose to guide your preparation.

    B. Structure the message by describing the problem, the solution, and the desired audience response and by adapting your persuasive approach, possibly with the *Motivated Sequence.*

    C. Use solid *evidence* by supporting claims and citing sources, and use *emotional evidence* if valid and appropriate.

    D. Avoid common *fallacies* that obstruct clear reasoning.

        1. attack on the person (*ad hominem*)

        2. reduction to the absurd (*reductio ad absurdum*)

        3. either-or

        4. false cause (*post hoc*)

        5. appeal to authority *(argumentum ad verecundiam)*

        6. bandwagon appeal *(argumentum ad populum)*

IV. Adapt to the *target audience* by establishing common ground, organizing for expected responses, and neutralizing potential hostility.

    A. Establish common ground with the audience by emphasizing shared values or mutual goals.

    B. Organize for expected responses from the audience.

    C. Neutralize potential hostility with understanding and humor.

V. Build *credibility* by understanding what it is and how to develop it with the three "c"s.

    A. Credibility is not objective; it is based on audience perception and may change from initial credibility to derived credibility to terminal credibility.

    B. Credibility is built by competence, character, and charisma.

Chapter 14 Summary

Persuasion is a part of our lives; we send and receive messages designed to influence. Persuasion is a communicative process that motivates someone to change a belief, behavior, or attitude. Usually this process does not happen quickly; instead, it is gradual, incremental, and interactive. Social judgment theory explains how someone's preexisting opinion or anchor can predict their latitudes of acceptance, rejection, and

ommitment. If you are proposing something that is within an audience's latitude of
eptance, or what they agree with, they will likely accept what you say. If you are
posing something that is within an audience's latitude of rejection, or what they
sagree with, then they will not accept what you are proposing. Finally, if you are
roposing something within their latitude of noncommitment, or what they don't have a
strong opinion about, then you have the best chance of changing their opinion to agree
with yours. Persuasion can be an ethical and effective way to stimulate, not coerce, others
to change a belief, an attitude, or a behavior. Ethical persuasion is truthful, not dishonest
or misleading, and it is in the best interest of the audience.

Persuasion has many facets. One way to categorize persuasive messages is by the
type of proposition presented to an audience. Propositions of fact try to convince others
that something is an actuality. Propositions of value attempt to persuade others what is
right or good. And propositions of policy try to sway others that certain courses of action
should be taken or that certain procedures should be in place. Persuasive efforts are also
categorized by end results or outcomes that are desired by the speaker. That end result
might be to convince others or to actuate others. The goal of convincing seeks internal
change in another's belief; no external or behavioral change needs to be evident. If the
persuader's goal is to actuate, he or she tries to move others to take action and behave in
a particular way. A speaker's goal may be to reinforce or strengthen a belief already held
by audience members rather than create a whole new belief. Finally, persuasion is
categorized by the approach of the persuader: direct or indirect. The former tells the
audience up front what the precise goal is, while the latter does not clearly state the
persuasive intent until later in the speech.

The nitty-gritty work of creating an effective persuasive message begins with
structuring a clear purpose statement that is specific, attainable, and focuses on what the
audience will be able to do at the end of your speech. Next, design your message so that
the audience is clear about the problem and the solution. If you're trying to move the
audience to action, you also need to state clearly to the audience what you want them to
do, whether that be to vote for a candidate, join an organization, write a letter, or stop
buying a product. Use both factual and emotional evidence ethically. Accurately cite your
sources. Search for and eliminate any of these common fallacies that undermine
credibility: personal attacks, reductions to the absurd, either-or, false cause, appeals to
authority, and bandwagon appeals.

Even the best constructed speech does not become a good presentation in a
vacuum. As the speaker, you need to adapt to your target audience, that core group of
people within the larger audience whom you are trying to persuade. Do this by
identifying and developing common ground with the audience, preparing for some
predictable responses, and trying to minimize potential hostility.

Finally, never take your credibility as a speaker for granted. Audiences may make
an initial assessment of your credibility, revise that by midspeech, and change their
assessment of you again by your conclusion. Several actions will help you build and

maintain your credibility. You must demonstrate competence by expertly researching your topic. Show character by being honest, trustworthy, and fair in your presentation. Finally, demonstrate charisma and magnetism by your enthusiasm. This advice should serve you well as you ethically and thoroughly prepare your persuasive presentation.

Chapter 14 Key Terms

For each of these terms, define the term, give an example, and explain the significance of the term.

1. actuate

2. *ad hominem* fallacy

3. anchor

4. *argumentum ad populum* fallacy

5. *argumentum ad verecundiam* fallacy

6. convince

7. credibility

8. direct persuasion

9. either-or fallacy

10. emotional evidence

11. ethical persuasion

12. evidence

13. fallacy

14. indirect persuasion

15. latitude of acceptance

16. latitude of noncommitment

17. latitude of rejection

18. Motivated Sequence

19. persuasion

20. *post hoc* fallacy

21. propositions of fact

22. propositions of policy

23. propositions of value

24. *reductio ad absurdum* fallacy

25. social judgment theory

26. target audience

Chapter 14 Review Questions

These questions are designed to help you understand this chapter's concepts and express your understanding in your own words. For practice with true/false and multiple-choice questions, use the CD-ROM you received with the text.

1. Choose one topic and give examples to illustrate the differences among propositions of fact, value, and policy. Then give examples to illustrate the differences between a goal of convincing and a goal of actuating.

2. What are the ethical questions involved in persuasion?

3. What is the importance of setting a clear persuasive purpose?

4. Why is it important to analyze and adapt to your audience?

5. Define the components of personal credibility.

Chapter 14 Thinking Outside the Box: Synthesizing Your Knowledge

These questions are designed to help you develop the big picture by blending what you've learned in this chapter and elsewhere.

1. How can the concepts you learned about listening (Chapter 4) help you be a better persuasive speaker?

2. Discuss and give examples of three precise ways that paying attention to principles of language (Chapter 3) can improve your speech. (Consider the uses of equivocal and relative words; facts, inference, and opinion; slang and jargon; high and low levels of abstraction.)

Chapter 14 Answers to Review Questions

1. Choose one topic and give examples to illustrate the differences among propositions of fact, value, and policy. Then give examples to illustrate the differences between a goal of convincing and a goal of actuating.

Answers will vary but will demonstrate the characteristics of each type of proposition. Propositions of fact try to convince the audience that something is true. Propositions of value try to convince the audience that something is good or bad, right or wrong. Propositions of policy try to convince the audience that something should be a practice or guideline.

On the topic of community service, three propositions illustrate the differences: Volunteers contribute to the well-being of a community (fact). It is good to have community service as a part of your life (value). All colleges should require forty hours of community service for graduation (policy). A speaker whose goal is to convince may speak to an audience of volunteers and want them to come away more convinced that their service is vital. A speaker with a goal to actuate may move an audience to sign up to participate in community service and act on their beliefs.

2. What are the ethical questions involved in persuasion?

The big questions are these: First, is the communication in the best interest of members of your audience? If your plan is one that would make life better for you but not for your audience, then it isn't ethical. Second, are you being honest? If you have falsified, distorted, or omitted crucial information, then your message is not ethical. In addition, honest expression of emotion without using emotion to cover for lack of evidence is the ethical path. Finally, citing your sources and not pretending that others' ideas or evidence are yours is a prime component of ethical persuasion.

3. What is the importance of setting a clear persuasive purpose?

It is easy to lose your way as you attempt to build your persuasive message. A clear purpose is like a beacon that helps you set your course and stay on course. If you have a clear purpose, you can be organized and coherent because you know the direction you want your message to go. A clear purpose guides you in organizing and developing your speech because both are directed toward your purpose.

4. Why is it important to analyze and adapt to your audience?

Each audience is unique, and to avoid having a canned effect, you must know the specific characteristics of the audience you are speaking to. Being able to identify your target audience (the subgroup you must persuade) allows you to focus your remarks for greatest effect. Audience analysis helps you understand what anchors and latitudes of acceptance, rejection, and noncommitment are probable. It allows you to emphasize the important values of the audience in order to make your point.

Adapting to your audience strengthens your rapport with the audience and increases the chances that the audience will find you to be logical and persuasive. Adaptation involves being prepared for the audience, whether they are hostile, favorable, or indifferent. By showing you understand the perspective of a hostile audience, you increase the chances that the audience will be willing to see your point of view. Adapting to the audience also means organizing according to the responses you expect from the audience to build on their goodwill and current beliefs.

5. Define the components of personal credibility.

A speaker gains credibility when he or she is viewed as having competence, character, and charisma. A speaker demonstrates competence with careful research, appropriate support, and a capable presentational manner. Character includes basic integrity, honesty, and fairness that result in your being trusted by the audience. Charisma refers to dynamism and likeability that an audience sees in you. Each of these—competence, character, and charisma—increases credibility.

Chapter 14 Answers to Thinking Outside the Box

1. How can the concepts you learned about listening (Chapter 4) help you be a better persuasive speaker?

*Listening helps in several tasks necessary for preparing a persuasive speech. Careful listening to the audience before speaking can help you understand what you have in common with the audience. It can also help you organize for expected responses from the audience. Careful listening will also help you understand the audience's anchors and latitudes of acceptance, rejection, and noncommitment. Understanding if your audience is **content, people, action,** or **time oriented** can help you structure your message to be received well. Review the principles of **critical listening** to understand how your audience may listen to assess your credibility and evaluate your evidence and appeals. [Boldfaced words are from Chapter 4.]*

2. Discuss and give examples of three precise ways that paying attention to principles of language (Chapter 3) can improve your speech. (Consider the uses of equivocal and relative words; facts, inference, and opinion; slang and jargon; high and low levels of abstraction.)

*Sample answers: Avoid **equivocal words** that can confuse the audience. Use precise terms and give additional details or information to clarify your meanings. Use numbers rather than **relative words**: "The country's average salary is $12,000," rather than, "It is a poor country." Clearly distinguish **factual statements** from **inferences** or **opinions**. Use words that are low on the **abstraction ladder** (concrete words) rather than high. For example, say "She received the Bronze Star and the Purple Heart," rather than, "She was a highly decorated veteran." In these ways, informative speeches give audiences more useful information.*

On the other hand, if you are trying to establish common ground with the audience, more abstract language may help you find places of agreement. ("We all agree that we want a better educated workforce," rather than, "We disagree on exactly who should pay for education.") [Boldfaced words are from Chapter 3.]